Th

Whistle

The Final Whistle

Midfield farewells, sudden deaths
and other strange but true passings
from football's history

Graham Sharpe

First published in Great Britain in 2001 by Robson Books,
10 Blenheim Court, Brewery Road, London N7 9NY

A member of the Chrysalis Group plc

British Library Cataloguing in Publication Data
A catalogue record for this title is available from the British Library

ISBN 1 86105 448 3

Typeset by SX Composing DTP, Rayleigh, Essex
Printed in Great Britain by Creative Print & Design (Wales), Ebbw Vale

CONTENTS

To my brother-in-law Bob Nelson, who will rest more happily in peace thanks to the kindness of his beloved Blackpool FC, who generously supplied some turf from Bloomfield Road which now adorns his grave.

INTRODUCTION

There is no easy way of explaining why I decided to tackle a subject which may well be considered to be in somewhat dubious taste – other than to admit that I believe I have identified a gap in the otherwise packed to the rafters library of football books.

Others have been too fearful of criticism, perhaps, to address the taboo subject of football fatalities. I have no wish to invite such adverse comment by appearing to be cashing in on tragedy and have no intention of dwelling on genuinely tragic events like Hillsborough, Heysel, the Manchester United air crash or the Bradford fire – although I do believe that it is worthwhile logging and recording these incidents.

Rather, in *The Final Whistle* the game-plan is to concentrate on the bizarre and fascinating element of football-related fatalities. The story which first set me thinking along these lines was the one about the Spanish fan who purchased a season ticket for his father as usual at the start of a new season, despite the fact that he was now a dead Dad, having expired during the close season. The plan was to reserve a seat and bring Dad's ashes along to the matches – the problems caused by this scheme are fully related in these pages.

There are a few dreadful puns along the way, and a number of tales which many may not wish to hear – they almost certainly won't buy the book. Included here is a unique day-by-day chronicle of fatal football facts, a short browse through which will serve to remind us that death is a fact of life for us all, without exception.

And then there are the stories which involve death in its many guises, but with an unexpected, unpleasant or unusual twist. We all have a healthy, if morbid, fascination for stories which leave us feeling grateful that there but for the grace of God, etc, etc and there are plenty of those on offer in these pages.

My unique survey into soccer club's attitudes to ash-scattering has proved to be a fascinating exercise and will help all fans to plan their ultimate resting place.

So if soccer suicides, murderous matches, passed-on players, funereal fans and fatal footballs strike something of a creepy chord within you, then prepare to visit football's dark side – that time beyond even extra time when the final whistle sounds, the game is over, and there can never be a replay.

Graham Sharpe

'To see families and friends scattering ashes of their loved ones on Goodison Park makes you realise that their devotion isn't just between three o'clock and five on a Saturday afternoon ...'

Former Everton and Scotland striker Graeme Sharp

I couldn't actually see him, but my Manchester United informant SOUNDED ashen-faced as he revealed, 'entirely off the record', to me that the Old Trafford club granted up to seventy requests per year for the ashes of deceased fans to be scattered at the Theatre of Dreams.

And he almost whispered to me, for fear of being overheard, 'We keep it quiet – or it could get out of hand.'

I wondered whether he meant that if it became widely known that ash-scattering was permitted by United it might lead to mass suicide by their supporters or that Euthanasia clubs would spring up to enable people to take advantage of this facility before a block went up.

I had clearly caused some concern and discussion in high places at United, by posing the question. They obviously didn't want to be perceived as being rude by not responding, but didn't want to divulge too much about this little discussed corner of life – or death.

Their City counterparts were not so shy, though – 'We

do organise the service', Katie Willis, their PR & Marketing Executive told me, in April 2001, 'It is available to any supporter or person wishing to do so. When the pitch was returfed last season we offered families pieces of the turf so that they could then be put on the deceaseds' gravestones. We will look to do this again when we move to the City of Estlands stadium in 2002/3.'

Whilst writing this book I had decided it would be fascinating to check out the attitudes of the senior football clubs in England, Scotland and Wales to ash-scattering requests, and I duly contacted every senior side – receiving responses from every Premiership club and many others.

I was right – there was a great variety of responses forthcoming – my favourite was Rochdale's, who revealed, 'We do permit it, but we usually ask those making the request whether they would mind not bringing all the ashes with them – have you ever seen the ashes of a deceased person? They can fill a shoe box.'

One wonders how many half empty, or half full shoe-boxes of ashes are still lurking around on top of TVs, tucked away in cupboards, or sitting next to fire grates in Rochdale homes, whilst those charged with disposing of them ponder where best to deposit the other half of Dad.

Rochdale reckon they receive three such requests a season on average – their spokeswoman told me she had previously worked for Oldham and Halifax, who had a similar rate – and usually request that when the ashes are scattered the person doing it should bring with them a priest or vicar to say a few words, 'because sometimes' she said, in a phrase which may not have been entirely what she'd intended, 'the person involved can go to pieces.'

A couple of issues associated with ash-scattering came up repeatedly. Notably, the problem of whether such a practice can have a detrimental effect on the playing surface, also whether it could offend players. Some clubs had dispensed with the process altogether as a result of such concerns, while others get around it by burying rather than scattering.

But Northampton Town, the second club to answer my letter, raised another question – 'The subject of scattering ashes on pitches has been debated recently and while a few clubs still permit this most have stopped due to Health and Safety regulations', Club secretary Norman W D Howells, F.C.C.A., claimed in his response of April 17, 2001.

Despite contacting health and safety officials I was unable to track down any such regulations. I was assured that ashes would present no health or hygiene problems, and were not subject to legislation until or unless buried.

He went on to tell me that Northampton, in association with the Council, 'have constructed a garden of rememberance and a number of ceremonies have taken place.'

Only Barnsley FC had been quicker to get back to me, with a more positive approach via General Manager, Michael Spinks – 'Our policy is to accommodate the requests of people who wish to have the ashes of a loved one scattered on the Oakwell pitch. In an average year we will have around four or five such ceremonies. Throughout my twenty three years with the Club we have accommodated every request which has been made to us and this policy will continue in the future.'

Some clubs do seem to fear an adverse effect on their grass – 'In previous years we did assist with such requests, but unfortunately the ashes seemed to react against the turf and caused scorch marks in the areas where they were scattered' said Bristol City's Rita Murgatroyd, PA to the Chairman. The club now 'agree, on the understanding that the ashes are only spread along the trackside and not on the pitch.'

Bradford City made a similar point, 'The only stipulation we have is that the ashes are not put on the actual playing surface as they tend to burn the grass,' said Secretary, Jon Pollard.

No such caveat at Albion Rovers FC, though – 'We have no problem with the scattering of ashes on the pitch,' said General Manager John Reynolds, adding, I detected, with a

touch of pride, or, indeed, glee, 'We allowed a family from England to scatter their father's ashes on the pitch.'

Hibernian have allocated an area to the rear of their Famous Five Stand goal, but 'ashes are not permitted to be scattered on the playing surface itself due to the detrimental effect it can have on the pitch, and the fact that many players object to the practice' according to Stadium Manager Garry O'Hagan.

A reason why they might object was supplied by Torquay United Director, Mike Bateson, 'We allowed ashes to be scattered until about ten years ago, when the practice was abandoned for reasons of taste. Many players objected to doing sliding tackles!'

Now Torquay 'allow the burial of ashes, usually interred near the touchline close to the deceased person's normal viewing spot. I would guess that we bury about a dozen per year.'

Many clubs, though, seem to be, ahem, dead set against this practice, 'We have over the years received a lot of requests for ashes to be scattered at our ground but it has not been permitted on the advice of our groundsmen. Next season we will relocate to a new stadium, but I have no reason to believe that our position will change' – Brian Truscott, Secretary of Southampton prior to their move from The Dell. So, a case of only Saints Alive there, then!

'We do not permit ceremonies for the scattering of deceased loved one's ashes, whether associated with the Club or not' declared Marlyn Hallam of Stirling Albion. Why not ? 'There is no particular reason for this and it was not introduced on any particular date, just a general decision made by the Board of Directors' was the response.

Glasgow Rangers confirmed that they no longer permitted ashes to be scattered, telling me that they had allowed it several years previously on an area of grass specifically set aside in a corner of their stadium, but that the area had since been 'filled in'. What became of that turf seemed to be unclear and the person designated to call me said that although they have no plans for a memorial garden, 'We do have a scheme where you can buy a brick with your name on it to be placed at the stadium.' Do you have to be dead to go on a brick? I asked. 'No,' was the cheery response.

Brighton & Hove Albion believe they are not in a position to accede to requests, 'due to the ground we are now playing at being owned by our local Council. We lease the ground and are unable to provide our supporters with any service of this nature' declared Chief Executive, Martin Perry.

Sheffield Wednesday would like to help, but can't always guarantee to do so: 'We do try to accommodate all requests, however, sometimes this is not always possible due to pitch renovation, etc.' confirmed Administration Manager, Sharon Lane.

Football League new boys Macclesfield Town were 'not aware that we have had any ashes scattered and there is no policy on this' but I felt a little sorry for poor old Berwick Rangers – if it isn't bad enough being an English-based club in the Scottish League, they also have to live with none of their supporters apparently being committed enough to want to rest in peace with them – despite having been in business since 1881! 'Please note, we have never in the past had any such requests' said Secretary Dennis McCleary, adding, rather ruefully, I felt, 'But I am sure we would look upon any individual case with a sympathetic hearing.'

Dunfermline Athletic are in a similar position, 'To date we have had no requests of this nature, but would be prepared to consider applications.'

Kidderminster Harriers could go one better: 'We have had one request that was adhered to, from a former Director of long association. Apart from this we would only consider the request under exceptional circumstances' said General Manager G H Butler.

A few clubs told me that their own Chaplains were available to deal with ash scattering duties.

Said Wolves' Rachael Heyhoe Flint, Director & PR

Executive, 'We are very happy to offer the facility for anyone associated with Wolves to have their remains placed at Molineux.

'We provide a brief service by our Club Chaplain, the Rev John Hall Matthews, who meets bereaved relatives and accompanies them through to the pitchside.

'Often relatives request a specific spot for the placing to coincide with the position of the deceased's seat in the stand.

'We also have Memorial Bricks placed in special sites on the various concourses of the stands, plus a Book of Remembrance sited in the Main Reception, Billy Wright stand, for relatives to further commemorate the link with Wolves of the deceased.

'Notices of bereavement can also be carried in our Match Day programme. Relatives are welcome to visit Molineux at any time to visit or view their commemorative sites.'

I would say that was a fully comprehensive service, wouldn't you? West Ham also 'allow scattering of ashes at our ground and provide the assistance of our Club Chaplain who normally conducts a brief prayer meeting before the ashes are scattered.'

Crystal Palace's Terry Byfield told me that their Chaplain, Nigel Sands, oversees ceremonies for them. I suspect few of them involve fans of their ground-share guests, Wimbledon.

I was most relieved that most approriately named of all clubs to be requested to answer my plea, Bury FC, responded via Secretary, Mrs J E Neville, 'We do permit scattering of ashes at our ground.'

As I completed my surevey, a quite extraordinary story emerged from Leeds United – where widow Wendy Moss, 36, arranged for husband Nigel's remains to be buried at Elland Road in August 2001. When the box containing his ashes was opened – it was empty!

Co-op Funeral Services were unable to explain where they had gone.

One point I raised in my letters to clubs was the question of what happened if they moved grounds. Would they be able to take the ashes with them, as it were – indeed, would someone whose desire it had been to be scattered at the ground where presumably they had spent their happiest hours, wish to be re-housed, as it were, elsewhere, albeit at the current location of their favourite team.

Perhaps this dichotomy is summed up best by the quandary in which a Mansfield Town fan's ashes are still resting. Christine Reynolds, Secretary at the Nottinghamshire club explains, 'Several years ago someone contacted us asking if she could spread her husband's ashes on the pitch. Just before she was due to do this she heard that we were probably either re-locating or re-developing the stadium.

'She then contacted us to say she would hold on to the ashes until the new stadium was built, as she did not want her husband's ashes to be 'moved' when the bulldozers came in.

'It has taken nearly five years to get the stadium finished.

'We are expecting a call any day from her.'

CLUB BY CLUB RESPONSES...

ABERDEEN FC... 'Aberdeen are happy to let ashes be scattered at Pittodrie. I would say that anyone is permitted to do this as unless you are a diehard supporter I do not see why you would want your ashes scattered here! We have had quite a few people's ashes scattered here and some families come here annually on the anniversary.' Caroline Calder, PR Co-ordinator.

AIRDRIEONIANS AFC... 'This has been done in the past, purely by request of the supporter's family and I assume that it will be carried out in the future, again only by request.'

ALBION ROVERS.. 'We have no problem with the scattering of ashes on the pitch.'

ARBROATH FC... 'We do allow the scattering of ashes at Gayfield.'

ARSENAL... estimated that up to one hundred enquiries a year are received by the Club – 'not all of them are followed up' – and told me that they are actively considering what, if any, action to take when and if a move from Highbury takes place. They have been taking soundings from people whose friends and relatives' ashes have been scattered there over the years as to whether they would prefer them left where they are or removed to the new ground when the time comes. 'The majority seem to be leaning towards leaving them where they are – after all, they are there because Highbury is where they wanted the ashes scattered, not at a new site.' The club has been building up a database of information about whose ashes are at the ground and have run stories in their programme. Meanwhile ceremonies and ash-scattering are still permitted at areas of the pitch near either the Clock End or North Bank.

ASTON VILLA... Aston Villa announced in 1996 that the

ashes of fans scattered on the Villa Park turf was causing damage to the grass and the practice was to be discontinued. However, in June 2001 in answer to my request for information about their policy, the club replied, 'We do occasionally allow the scattering of ashes on the pitch in special circumstances' adding, 'May I suggest you write to the Chairman with your request and he will consider it and respond to you' – they must have thought I wanted myself scattered at Villa Park.

BARNET FC... 'We do not have any hard and fast rule. In the time I have been with the club we have twice been asked if it would be possible to scatter ashes and because they were both ardent fans our Chairman allowed their families and church representatives to do so. I feel that if they were not regular supporters that had a strong affiliation with the Club then he would probably have declined.' Beverley Bacon, Office Administration.

BARNSLEY... Policy is 'to accommodate the requests of people who wish to have the ashes of a loved one scattered on the Oakwell pitch.'

BERWICK RANGERS... 'Since you ask, no one has asked in 120 years.'

BIRMINGHAM CITY... 'Fans can have their ashes scattered at the ground,' said managing director Karren Brady to the News of the World in March 2001, also announcing a new gold, silver and bronze funeral service for supporters – 'The coffin is decorated in Birmingham City colours and the service is conducted in a hospitality suite.' The club also offers a book of remembrance at the stadium.

BLACKBURN ROVERS... Their PR man, Paul Agnew told me that he believed the Premiership frowned on the scattering of ashes on pitch surfaces and told me that Blackburn received some 25-30 requests per year and permitted all of them, with Club chaplain Ken Howells happy to help out when required. 'The ashes are scattered on a section left for the purpose at the Blackburn end of the ground between the running track and the pitch.'

BLACKPOOL FC... 'We do not permit ashes to be scattered at Bloomfield Road but we do bury them in a shallow space behind the goals.However, this practice has been put on hold due to the redevelopment of the ground. I have suggested that maybe engraved plaques could be attached to the back of seating in the stands.' Carole Banks, Secretary.

BOLTON WANDERERS... 'We do permit the scattering of ashes by prior arrangement, but we don't receive that many requests, I can only recall a couple over the past season or two' said a Press Office spokesman in June 2001.

BRADFORD CITY... 'Yes, but not on playing surface.'

BRIGHTON & HOVE ALBION... 'No can do as we only lease the ground from the Council.'

BRISTOL CITY... Used to allow unrestricted scattering; then discouraged requests; now 'agree on the understanding that the ashes are only spread along the trackside.'

BRISTOL ROVERS... 'We do permit ashes ceremonies at The Memorial Stadium – but as the ground is shared with Bristol Rugby Club we may also have requests from their supporters and ex-players.'

BURNLEY... 'Maintains a policy that ashes cannot be scattered at Turf Moor, but we do allow supporters to scatter a deceased loved one's ashes at Gawthorpe, which is the club's training ground. I understand that the ashes can scorch the turf.' Cathy Pickup, Company Secretary.

BURY FC... 'We do permit scattering of ashes at our ground.'

CELTIC... 'The Club previously allowed supporters to scatter ashes behind the goal-line at Celtic Park but this practice was stopped a number of years ago, after the stadium was redeveloped. We now have in place a Book of Remembrance in which supporters can enter a message and/or photograph on behalf of their deceased relative.' Clare McGee, Public Relations Assistant.

CHARLTON ATHLETIC... When Charlton were temporarily away from The Valley funeral processions and corteges would drive around the derelict ground. Now that they are back there permanently they are happy to invite people to take advantage of their Garden of Remembrance, and offer the services of the Club chaplain.

CHELSEA... I spoke to a charming and sympathetic lady who told me that she often had to 'try not to cry' when people visited Stamford Bridge to scatter the ashes of their loved ones. 'We always allow it, and often receive thank-you cards from grateful relatives,' she said. 'We check with the ground staff first that there is no activity taking place on or around the pitch and arrange for it to happen from Monday to Friday but not on match days. Staff dig a hole to allow the burial of ashes to take place and a plaque can be put up in the concourse. We make no charge for the facility.' The same lady explained that she had only recently helped out with a heart-rending case when a lady scattered the ashes of her thirty-year-old son at the ground and estimated that she dealt with around four cases a month on average. Former right half Ken Armstrong's ashes were scattered here in 1984 when he died, aged 60.

CHELTENHAM TOWN... 'We treat such requests very sympathetically and do allow informal ceremonies to take place in private.'

COVENTRY CITY FC... 'Our Club does permit the ashes of any of our deceased supporters to be spread on the cinder track surrounding our playing surface.'

COWDENBEATH... Told me that they had only ever had one such request, to which they acceded.

CRYSTAL PALACE FC... 'We do permit the scattering of deceased ashes onto a particular area of grass behind our Holmesdale Road Stand.'

DERBY COUNTY... The club had banned the scattering of ashes at The Baseball Ground in recent years, but since their move to a new stadium, Club groundsman Mark Robinson is happy to offer a service to those who request it, although he asks that relatives should wait until November or December as he believes that conditions at that time of year ensure that there is little danger of damaging the playing surface if ashes are scattered either in the goalmouths or the centre of the pitch. 'We had five such requests last year at Pride Park.' Mr Robinson recalled in summer 2001.

DUNDEE FC... 'Dundee FC deal sympathetically with requests, and have not had to turn down any in recent memory.'

DUNFERMLINE ATHLETIC... 'Would be prepared to consider applications.'

EAST FIFE FC... 'We have allowed the scattering of a deceased loved one's ashes at our ground in the past.'

EVERTON... 'I like to say that we encourage rather than permit people to scatter the ashes of deceased supporters at Goodison' said Lesley Bradley. Everton were the only club to tell me that such ceremonies were normally carried out on one specific day – a Tuesday. 'During the season there is probably at least one ceremony a week.' The Club has its own chaplain but allows people to bring their own priest, etc if preferred. 'We used to bury the ashes until recently, but have now set aside an area for scattering at the edge of the playing surface.'

FALKIRK FC... 'We do permit the scattering of ashes at our

Ground and this is for anyone involved with the Club.' Sarah Scott, Commercial Manager.

FORFAR ATHLETIC... 'We have these requests say perhaps once every couple of years and we never have any problem in acceding.'

FULHAM... 'We always allow it – indeed the Club Reverend Gary Piper is happy to assist – even if it is not a religious ceremony,' I was told, having e-mailed the club for details. 'We allow as many or as few people to attend the ceremony as requested and have set aside an area behind a goal. We would certainly never say no and have around fourteen requests per year.'

GLASGOW RANGERS... No longer able to permit scattering.

HALIFAX TOWN.. 'Such requests would be considered on individual merits.'

HEART OF MIDLOTHIAN FC... 'We do allow the scattering of ashes at our ground.'

HIBERNIAN... Permit ashes scattering 'in a limited location', not on the playing surface. When levelling works took place on the pitch, the Club 'was careful to remove the top half inch of the surface before returning it on completion of the works.'

HUDDERSFIELD TOWN... 'We do allow the scattering of ashes, behind the goal area only.'

INVERNESS CALEDONIAN THISTLE... 'All situations will be considered on their individual merits.'

IPSWICH TOWN... 'The club does allow supporters' ashes to be buried outside the pitch area and would naturally accede to any player/director request for the same.'

KIDDERMINSTER HARRIERS FC... Only had one request – it was granted.

KILMARNOCK FC... 'The club have no set policy on this matter but we consider each request on its merits. The timing of the request, the condition of the pitch may have a bearing on our response.'

LEEDS UNITED... used not to offer a service having previously done so, but have now set an area aside at the north end of their ground at which they permit the burying of urns, their Press Office told me.

LEICESTER CITY... whose telephone switchboard takes you through a menu of seven options – none of them concerning ash scattering – before permitting you to speak to a human being (I think she was, anyway) who told me that the Club Chaplain was available to assist with such requests and that people only needed to ring to make arrangements. They have an area near one of the goalmouths set aside for the purpose.

LIVERPOOL... 'We do permit only the scattering of ashes, anywhere on the pitch. We don't reveal the precise number of such requests we receive per year, but there are quite a few.' Actor Ricky Tomlinson wishes his ashes to be scattered at Anfield.

LIVINGSTON FC... 'We do permit such ceremonies. We have had and fulfilled several requests of this nature over the years and will continue to do so.'

LUTON TOWN... 'With regard to ashes, due to the chemicals now used in cremation we can no longer spread them on the pitch. As we anticipate moving within the next two to three years we will not be putting any more ashes on the site. However, it is anticipated that we will have a small remembrance garden at the new stadium where all our deceased supporters will be remembered and their ashes placed.' Cherry Newberry, Club Secretary.

MACCLESFIELD TOWN... 'I'm not aware that we have had any ashes scattered. There is no policy on this.'

MANCHESTER CITY... Service 'available to any supporter or person wishing to do so.'

MANSFIELD TOWN... Do permit scattering.

MIDDLESBROUGH... 'We don't allow it at the moment, but are considering a Garden and Book of Remembrance. We have not permitted the scattering of ashes since moving in to the Riverside Stadium.'

MILLWALL... Have opened a Memorial Garden to serve such requests, also providing memorial plaques at the club concourse. Dean Wilson, who is responsible for organising such events runs Sports Memorials UK in association with Millwall and hopes to expand it to more clubs. Solid granite black plaques are available at a cost of £138 at time of going to press. He recalled once 'taking the cortege through the ground on the day of a funeral.'

MOTHERWELL FC... 'We have, in the past, had only a few requests for such a ceremony and on the occasions in question the deceased have been closely connected with the club, ex-players, groundsmen, lifelong supporters etc. The requests therefore have been grated [sic – a Freudian slip?] in these instances.' Lynne McKay, PA to General Manager.

NEWCASTLE... 'We do allow for people to come into the ground to scatter ashes, but not on the pitch, they can only scatter them on the perimeter path that goes around the pitch. Debbie Wiggins deals with the requests. She arranges for them to come into the stadium, normally on a Sunday or when there is no game being played,' says Vicky Walmsley, Media & PR assistant. 'War Jackie Milburn', scorer of 238 goals in 492 games for the club, died aged 64 in 1988 and his ashes were scattered at the ground.

NORTHAMPTON TOWN... Ceremonies permitted in garden of remembrance.

NOTTS COUNTY... 'We only receive a small number of requests in respect of the scattering of deceased loved ones' ashes at our ground, and people are made aware that we cannot be held responsible for any future ground development or alterations to our pitch or Stadium.'

PETERBOROUGH UNITED... 'The Posh have allowed the scattering of ashes for its supporters for as long as can be remembered.'

PLYMOUTH ARGYLE... 'Yes.'

RAITH ROVERS... 'Our club does permit the scattering of ashes of supporters and relatives of supporters at our ground.'

READING... 'We do allow ashes to be scattered at Madejski Stadium. It is something we used to do at our old Elm Park ground, and have continued with since moving here in 1988', Andy West, PR Officer

ROCHDALE... 'Okay, but please don't bring all the ashes.'

ROTHERHAM UNITED... 'We do permit the scattering of ashes on our ground and we normally do it for any one who requests it'. P Henson, Chief Executive.

SCUNTHORPE UNITED FC... 'We receive a number of requests for people to scatter their deceased loved one's ashes and are quite happy to allow this providing it is not on a matchday. We have also received requests to place a plaque in memory of the deceased and we have designated a specific area for this purpose.'

SHEFFIELD WEDNESDAY... 'We do try to accommodate all requests.'

SOUTHAMPTON FC... 'Not permitted on the advice of our groundsmen.'

SOUTHEND UNITED... 'We do allow the scattering of ashes which can only be scattered in certain areas, ie, not on the pitch itself.'

STENHOUSEMUIR FC... 'Re: The scattering of loved ones' ashes – I write to advise that we would have no objections to this request.' D.O. Reid, Secretary.

STIRLING ALBION... 'We do not permit ceremonies for the scattering of deceased loved one's ashes.'

ST JOHNSTONE FC... 'I would advise that it is my club's practice to accede to requests to permit the scattering of a deceased's ashes at our ground and this extends to former directors, players, supporters, etc'. Stewart Duff, Managing Director.

STOKE CITY... 'Our policy is that each individual case will be reviewed and requests should be made in writing.' Nicki Yates, Public Relations Officer. The ashes of Sir Stanley Matthews were reportedly buried under centre spot.

SUNDERLAND FC... 'We have a section at the side of the pitch where we allow bereaved families to bury ashes beneath a small section of turf.'

SWANSEA CITY... 'We have allowed supporters to scatter their loved ones' ashes at the ground. In the past three years this has occurred on four occasions.'

TORQUAY UNITED... 'We do allow the burial of ashes near the touchline.'

TOTTENHAM HOTSPURS... 'The facility was stopped a few years back – we no longer do it because of the numbers involved. I certainly do not know of any plans to introduce a Garden or Book of Remembrance, or commemorative plaques.' I was told by the Club's Press Office.

WALSALL FC... 'A slab of turf is removed, outside the goal-line area, the ashes scattered into the soil,and the turf put

back into position. Pitch renovation, or pitch reconstruction may well lead to the ashes being disturbed.' K.R.Whalley, Secretary.

WATFORD FC... The club has two Chaplains who organise ceremonies – John Graham, and Rev Andrew D. Cowley.

WEMBLEY STADIUM... I was reliably informed from two separate sources who worked at the Stadium that ashes scattered at the Stadium were put on the greyhound track – oh well, we all end up going to the dogs in one way or another.

WEST HAM... Allow scattering.

WIGAN ATHLETIC AFC... 'We do allow the ashes of loved ones to be buried on the pitch, but do not scatter them. When we moved from Springfield Park (to JJB Stadium) loved ones asked for pieces of the pitch.'

WIMBLEDON... 'We used to permit it at Plough Lane but I can assure you there is no way supporters would want to be scattered at Selhurst Park where we currently groundshare, so such a facility is now in abeyance.' Club spokesman.

WOLVERHAMPTON WANDERERS... Allow pitch-side scattering.

WYCOMBE WANDERERS FC... 'The club do accede where there is a connection with the Club, such as regular supporters, for ashes to be scattered only on the grass areas either behind or alongside the goals.'

YORK CITY FC... 'The Club does not allow scattering of ashes on our ground. We do, however, allow ashes to be deposited in a hole.'

AERIAL ACTIVITY

Comic Rod Hull died in March 1999 after complaining that the TV reception for the match he was watching between Manchester United and Inter Milan was poor because the aerial needed adjusting. The 63-year-old climbed up on to the roof of his home, only to slip and fall to his death on to the roof of a greenhouse.

ASHES

The dying wish of a fan of Spanish side Betis Sevilla was that he could continue to support his beloved team – even from beyond the grave. Rather than sprinkle his father's ashes around the ground, his son decided to renew his dad's club membership – and then to take him to home matches in a glass urn. This upset club security stewards, it was revealed in November 1995, when officials suggested that the fan leave his father's ashes in the Sevilla trophy room. This suggestion, in turn, upset club cleaning staff, who objected to the 'morbid atmosphere' it would create. So a compromise was reached, permitting the son to bring the father to games in a cardboard container, described as 'a sort of milk carton', which was placed on a seat to allow a clear view of the game. 'Every time Betis scores,' said the anonymous son, 'I give him a little shake.'

Joshua Walter Sloan, known as Paddy, was a centre forward who played for many clubs including Tranmere, Fulham, Arsenal and Sheffield Utd then abroad for Brescia, Torino, Udinese and Rabat Ajax of Malta, also coaching in Australia where he died aged 72 on 7 January, 1993. However, widow Barbara was determined to honour his wish of having his ashes buried at Highbury – he played 33 games for Arsenal – and the club duly agreed.

The ashes of great British football administrator and FIFA President, Sir Stanley Rous, who died in July 1986, were scattered over a football pitch at Mutford, near Lowestoft, the village where he was born.

Interviewed during 2000, Ian Wright was asked where he wanted his ashes scattered: 'Half at Highbury, half at White Hart Lane,' he replied.

West Ham's priest conducts services on the centre spot, remembering the person who has died, scattering a minimal amount of ash in the centre circle, the rest around the outside of the pitch.

When Ajax moved stadiums in 1996, a large section of their old pitch was dug up and replanted at the nearby Westgaarde cemetery and crematorium. Here, for approx £100, ashes can be scattered, and red and white plaques

commemorating the dead erected.

Asked by London's ES magazine "Where in London would you have your ashes scattered" in May 2001, Sol Campbell replied, "The West Ham ground, Upton Park. It's where it all started for me, so it would be a good place for it all to finish."

ASSASSINATION

President of Albanian title challengers Tomori Berat, Adrian Cobo, and FIFA referee Luan Zylfo were shot dead in summer 2000, when a gunman walked into Partizani Tirana's stadium where Tomori had just played a League game, and shot Cobo five times in the head. Zylfo was hit in the neck and died in hospital.

AYATOLLAH

Bizarrely, Cardiff City fans showed an empathy with the good folk of Iran when their religious leader the Ayatollah Khomeini died. Inspired by TV footage of grieving Iranians slapping their heads in despair, the City fans, struggling at the time, did likewise, whilst singing 'Do the Ayatollah, Do the Ayatollah, Ner ner ner ner.'

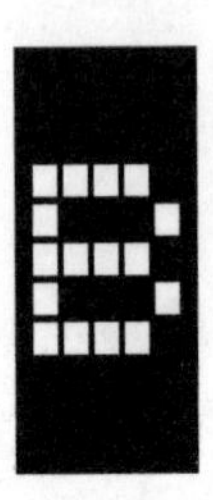

BAN

Football was banned completely in Mauritius in 1999 after seven people died at a stadium as a result of a fire started on the terraces. The ban was lifted seven months later.

BATS ON

Andy Ducat, who played for Woolwich, Arsenal, Aston Villa and Fulham and won six England caps, was also a Surrey cricketer in 1906–31, and an England international, who collapsed and died in July 1942 with a bat in his hand whilst playing for Surrey Home Guard against their Sussex equivalent at Lord's.

BEDICATED

Football League and Scottish League clubs found an unexpected way of remembering League founder William McGregor's 1911 death – they endowed Birmingham Hospital with the McGregor Bed.

BEREAVEMENT

In 1884 Vale of Leven reached the Scottish Cup Final, but refused to play when the Scottish FA would not let them postpone the date because of injury and family bereavement – so they just let Queens Park have the trophy.

BOMBED

Bombs fell on Sunderland's Roker Park in March 1943, hitting the pitch and killing a policeman.

BOOKED

Chris Hulme's Yellow Jersey Press-published *Manslaughter United* tells the true story of a group of murderers and wardens making up Kingston Arrows prison team. Their 1997–98 side in the Portsmouth North End League included nine convicted murderers – they played only home games.

Joe McGinnis's superb *The Miracle of Castel di Sangro* which, in my humble opinion as organiser of the event, was unlucky not to win the William Hill Sports Book of the Year Award when it was short-listed, tells the story of a referee hanged by fans of a team called Celano in the late seventies, after making a series of terrible decisions.

McGinnis, an American spending a year following an obscure Italian side, is appalled: 'Was anyone arrested?' he asks.

'Oh no. The police, the magistrates in Rome, they all knew that the referee had been at fault.'

During Joe's stay with the Serie B side two of their players, Danilo Di Vincenzo and Filippo Biondi, are tragically killed.

The Day Italian Football Died, written by Alexandra Manna and Mike Gibbs and published by Breedon Books, tells the story of the events leading up to, and the aftermath of, the 1949 air disaster in which 31 people were killed – including the entire Torino team, as well as reserves, training staff and directors. They had recently won three Serie A titles and provided most of the international side.

James Sharpe's bizarre *The Bewitching of Anne Gunter*, published by Profile Books in 1999, is a 'horrible and true story of football, witchcraft, murder and the King of England' and concerns a feud which began in 1598 'when Brian Gunter had inflicted fatal injuries on two of the Gregorys at a football match.'

Quizzed on his favourite reading matter, England and West Ham keeper David James named a book by forensic psychologist, John Douglas, *Journey into Darkness*, in which the author analyses serial killers and psychopaths.

BOOTS ON

Blackpool fan Andy Sharples, 43, collapsed and died as his side's striker Brett Ormeroyd scored two minutes from time in the 4-2 3rd Division play-off final victory against Leyton Orient in May 2001 at Cardiff's Millennium Stadium. Said son Karl 'He lived long enough to hear the final whistle, and died a happy man.'

BUDGIE

Striker Stan Collymore's well-publicised problems with stress and depression could well have had their roots in a

1996 incident in which he was accused by a Newcastle fan of killing a pet budgerigar. The supporter, Dominic Hourd, wrote to Collymore – then playing for Liverpool – after he scored a late winner, causing Hourd and his friend Peter Phillips to kick out in frustration, knocking the budgie's cage off its stand and causing its demise. 'He can't bring Peter the Budgie back,' said Hourd, 'but I told him I couldn't forgive him for what he did.'

When ref Hamid Rissaoui was requested by East Grinstead League side The Crown's skipper Phil Jarman to permit a minute's silence before kick off in their April 2001 game against Stone Quarry, he saw no reason to refuse. So Hamid called the players together around the centre circle and blew for sixty seconds' silence, which was impeccably observed. When one of the players was spotted giggling Rissaoui made enquiries about who had passed away – 'Jarman said a member of his family had died.' The ref was not best pleased when it was revealed that the family member was Jarman's pet budgie.

BULL

Napoleon the Bull, Hereford United's mascot, who was paraded before the crowd at Cup ties, was tragically put down at the age of four in February 2000 – after being injured whilst performing mating duties with a heifer. A suggestion that the bull should be eaten at a celebration dinner was reportedly described as 'in the worst possible taste' by club officials.

CAR CRASH

Brazilian star striker Edmundo was sentenced to four and a half years for killing three people in a 1995 car crash.

CEMETERY

Celtic's North Stand was opened in August 1995, featuring an upper tier cantilevered out to the rear, overhanging a cemetery. The club had to pay £10,000 to the council as compensation to the residents of said cemetery, now deprived of their promised air 'from the centre of the earth to the sky'.

England striker Kevin Phillips once woke up 'on a dead person'. Gary Roberts, then manager of Baldock Town of the Doc Martens League, and a team mate of Phillips' when he played for that club, recalled, 'Kev was a top bloke, but he once fell asleep in a cemetery – on someone's gravestone. It was after a heavy club night at the end of the season, and I remember a couple of the lads were struggling to get home.

Kevin couldn't quite work out where he was or what was going on, so he decided to get his head down for a while. He got a bit of a shock the next morning when he woke up on top of a dead person.'

Romania were not best pleased when they were allocated a training pitch next to a cemetery prior to a 1998 game away to Greece. 'It is not very pleasant playing next door to crosses and tombs,' said defender Anton Dobos – a man from the land of Dracula!

Romanian side Astra Ploiesti turned up for training at a new site leased to them by the local council – only to discover body parts pushing through to the playing surface. They had been allocated a cemetery. 'It is particularly bad in the rain,' complained manager Ion Radu in August 2000. 'We have found everything from a skull to false teeth.'

CENTENARIANS

Zecharia March was believed to be the oldest surviving former professional footballer when he died in September 1994, weeks before his 102nd birthday, which fell on 25 October. He played for Brighton and Portsmouth.

CHAIRY OF DEATH

Southampton were banned from selling off seats from The Dell when they moved grounds – because they contained toxins which could be potentially fatal – if anyone sucked or ate them!

COFFIN

Undertaken with Love, a newly created company in Cleveland, launched its funeral business in December 1998 by offering football fans the opportunity of being buried in club-coloured coffins.

An Isle of Wight undertaker began offering coffins in football colours in June 1996, reported *The Guardian*.

Artist Carol Aston introduced a new service for Shropshire residents in November 1999 – the hand painting of coffins in the colours of the deceased's favourite club, at her base, the Craven Arms pub.

In November 1998 *The Guardian* revealed that 'a funeral company in Rio de Janeiro is doing a booming trade in customised coffins for local football nuts' which are produced in a range of club colours, complete with crest. For an extra charge they will also arrange to bury the deceased in team kit.

Portsmouth fans carried a coffin to their Fratton Park ground before their January 1999 win over Huddersfield, to symbolise their determination to keep the club alive despite going into administration.

Playing their final game at Brockville Park at the end of the 1999–2000 season, Falkirk supporters dressed as undertakers carried a coffin on to the pitch before a half time penalty shoot-out – at the end of which the coffin opened and a 'corpse' jumped out to score from the spot.

Since the 1950s Preston North End has traditionally marked relegation by the ceremonial laying to rest of a coffin in the cellar of the Witney Trees pub – with promotion heralding the lifting of the coffin, which is carried to the nearby Trades Hall.

Coffins in Bayern Munich colours went on sale for £3,500 in October 1997.

CORPSE CURE

Bristol Rovers midfielder Jamie Shore, 21, and John Salako were amongst the first players to benefit from a new technique when cartilage and ligament extracted from corpses was used in operations to repair knee damage in late summer 1999.

CORPSE-NAPPER

The body of former Nigerian soccer skipper Sam 'Zagallo' Opone was held to ransom by a witch doctor, claiming that he had not been paid for treatment given to the player, reported *The Daily Telegraph*. Opone was treated by Blacky Awommi after suffering a stroke in 1999 and becoming paralysed. The healer ceased treatment, claiming that he had received no payment, and the former defender died. In April 2001 former Nigeria FA official Austin Akosa said: 'The herbalist has threatened the player's son that he will use magic to kill him if he does not come up with the money.' Opone's son, Lucky (!) said: 'I'm yet to see my father's corpse, having only read about his death in the newspapers.'

DEAD CERT

A Vietnamese punter was killed after brawls broke out between gamblers placing illegal bets on Euro 2000 in Ho Chi Minh City, said local reports at the time.

DEAD CROSS

Following four consecutive defeats, players at the Italian Third Division club Viterbese were shocked to discover eleven wooden crosses, each bearing the name of a different player, planted in the middle of their pitch, in January 1997. The stunt had the desired effect when the team won their next match, against Sicily's Juveterranova 1–0, but skipper Massimiliano commented: 'We played with death in our hearts.'

It was reported that when FC Bruges clinched the Belgian championship in 1990 their fans 'celebrated by hurling billiard balls at the police, along with crosses stolen from a cemetery.'

DEAD-END JOB

Hanging up his boots at the end of his World Cup winning career, England left back Ramon 'Ray' Wilson went into a funeral business in Huddersfield.

DEADLY CONNECTIONS

Between movie murderer Hannibal Lecter and footballer Julian Joachim – who is glimpsed playing for Leicester on a TV during the film *Hannibal*.

Between Admiral Horatio Nelson and Blackpool FC – the naval legend is said to haunt the Bloomfield Road club's boardroom, where wood from Nelson's ship *Foudroyant* was used in panelling.

Between the Pope and Charlton keeper Dean Kiely – one of whom wishes to die and return in a future life as the other.

DEATH BED TRANSFER

Liverpool were set to splash out their record fee – an unheard of £75 – in the 1880s for Preston North End striker Jimmy Ross, a Scot who had proved his ability with eight goals in their 26–0 thrashing of Hyde in an FA Cup game. But Ross's older brother Nick, a star with Everton and Preston, was not keen that his brother should move to Anfield, and when he, Nick, was taken seriously ill he pleaded on his death bed with Jimmy to stay with Preston. Agonising over his decision Jimmy finally plumped for the switch to Liverpool, where he eventually played 78 League games and became skipper. He died in 1902, when he was still on the books of Manchester City.

DEAD FUNNY

The ref met his priest and asked him whether he thought there would be football in heaven. 'Well, there's good news and bad news,' said the priest. 'The good news is that there is indeed football in heaven. The bad news is – you're down for a game next Saturday.'

DEATH OF FOOTBALL

After a legal challenge to reinstate the prohibited traditional annual street football game in Ashbourne, Derbyshire, was lost in 1860, a handbill purporting to be an Obituary for the Right Honourable Game Football was issued:

> It becomes our painful duty to record the death of the Right Honourable Game of Football, which melancholy event took place in the Court of Queen's Bench on Wednesday, 14 November, 1860. The deceased Gentleman was, we are informed, a native of Ashbourne, Derbyshire, at which place he was born in the Year of Grace 217, and was consequently in the 1643rd year of his age. For some months the patriotic Old Man had been suffering from injuries sustained in his native town. His untimely end has cast a gloom over the place, where the amusement he afforded the inhabitants will not soon be forgotten.

DEATH ROW

Barcelona vice-president Nicolau Causus spent 72 days on death row in cell number 338 of Barcelona's Modelo prison during the Spanish Civil War. His sentence was later commuted and he was still with Barcelona at time of writing.

DEATH THREAT

Perhaps the first football-related death threat was recorded in 1886 when Berwick Rangers lost 1–0 to a side called Royal Oaks, a team of fishermen who took the lead when their centre forward threatened Rangers' keeper Cleghorn with 'If you stop the ball I'll kill you.' After the match Cleghorn confirmed 'He would ha' done it.'

German club 1860 Munich's President Karl-Heinz Wildmoser received death threats from fans angered by plans to ground-share with neighbours Bayern in March 2001. 'I have received death threats – yes, death threats. I am scared. However, I am 120kgs of living dynamite. If there is anybody who wants to kill me I will take him with me!'

Former Middlesbrough defender Christian Ziege, who had moved to Liverpool, revealed that 'A few idiots have adorned my house in Middlesbrough with rotten eggs. There was also a murder threat in the mailbox.'

'Look at me linesman, I want you to recognise my face, because the next time you see it will be the moment you're going to die' . . . Charming comment from a Millwall supporter to top ref David Elleray, recalled in the TV programme, *Man In Black: Confessions of a Whistle Blower*, screened by Channel 4 in July 2000.

'When I heard about the death threat on Brooklyn I had sympathy for David. I hate him because he plays for Manchester United, but that threat was below the belt' . . . Oasis star and Manchester City fan Liam Gallagher on the threats made to Posh and Becks's child, Brooklyn, in February 2000.

Threats were still being received by Maurice Johnston, who was transferred from Celtic to Rangers, even in March 2000 when he was living in Kansas City, USA, playing for local side the Wizards.

Threats were received by pub landlord Chris Teague of Yates' Wine Lodge, Swansea, in June 2000 after he offered free beer every time opponents scored against England in Euro 2000.

Threats were received by 78-year-old FIFA delegate Charles Dempsey, the New Zealander whose failure to cast a vote on who should stage the World Cup in 2006 in the July 2000 voting process handed the honour to Germany. His failure to vote for South Africa, as instructed, lost them a share of the decision.

After accusing Italy of cheating to win the 1934 World Cup, respected German football statistician Dr Alfredo Poge was issued with a death threat by Italian terrorist group *Fiamme Nere* – the Black Flames. Bribery and the fielding of ineligible players were amongst the claims of Poge, who said, 'It is hard for Italians to accept that corruption was involved in their triumph. The second leg of the qualifying tie between Italy and Greece was never held. Four members of the Greek team told us the Italians built a house in Athens for the Greek FA in return for them conceding the match. The Swedish referee Ivan Eklind gave the fascist salute to Mussolini before taking charge of the Final and I believe he was sympathetic to the Italian team.'

DEDICATED

Motherwell dedicated its New Stand, opened in May 1995, to former player Davie Cooper who was with them from 1989–94 but died at the age of 39, three weeks after the stand opened. Clydebank, where Cooper began his career, named their stadium in his honour.

DI DAY

On the afternoon of Saturday, 6 September, 1997, the day of the funeral of Diana, Princess of Wales, it was possible to shop at supermarkets, or Selfridges; to visit a theme park; buy a National Lottery ticket or a Big Mac. It was not, though, possible to watch football, play football or place a bet on a football match. There had been no Premiership matches scheduled anyway, but the football authorities called off all League matches at senior level. Scotland's World Cup qualifier against Belarus was to have taken place that afternoon, but an avalanche of criticism, and threats by players not to take part, saw the game switched to Sunday.

Andy Mitchell, Head of Media Relations at the Scottish Football Association, later reflected: 'A morning funeral and an afternoon fixture did not seem to us to conflict. But, just to be sure, the SFA made high level contact with as many relevant bodies as possible.' FIFA told the SFA, 'The match should go ahead with all the normal marks of respect, such as a minute's silence and flags at half mast.' Planning to play the game, Mitchell said, 'Perhaps we were so busy that nobody foresaw the hysteria that would mount so forcefully and quickly against the SFA.' On the Tuesday before the game Mitchell said that the Lord Chamberlain's Office 'was of the view that provided the match did not conflict directly with the funeral service then there was no protocol problem with the match taking place, and he added "Life goes on".'

Not if the media had anything to do with it, it didn't. After what Mitchell described as 'an extraordinary example of nationwide hype, indignation and moral outrage' the game was postponed until the Sunday. Given my interest in both football and betting I wrote at the time: 'I fully accept that many people found it distasteful that there should be any commercial activity whatsoever that afternoon; but I object to the implicit suggestion that football and betting should be unacceptable whereas other, equally profit-orientated operations – not excluding the very media which co-ordinated the campaign to have football and betting shut down – were able to trade without organised disapproval.'

(DIED WITH THEIR) BOOTS ON

Leeds were 0–1 down at home to Burnley in their Second Division game on 27 October, 1906. At half time, centre forward David Wilson, a heavy-smoking former Boer War soldier who had seen active service, complained of not feeling too well. He went out for the second half but soon had to leave the pitch. With no substitutes available in those days Wilson returned to the pitch, but after only two more minutes had to go off again – and died shortly after in the dressing room.

Hibs' full back James Main died in December 1909, four days after being kicked in the stomach during a match.

Luton Town full back Sammy Wightman was kicked in the stomach during a Southern League match at Brighton on 8 April, 1912 – Easter Monday. At first it seemed he was only winded, but he later went off. After the match he was passed fit to travel by a doctor but became ill on the train home and

was rushed to hospital where, after an operation, he never regained consciousness and died on 10 April.

Former Woolwich Arsenal player Bob Benson turned up as a spectator to watch his old side take on Reading in a 1916 wartime match. Bob, 33, was persuaded to put his boots on and take part, despite not having played since retiring two seasons earlier – it was a fatal decision as his lack of fitness told and he was helped from the pitch in clear distress then died minutes later in the dressing room. He was buried in an Arsenal shirt.

Dumbarton keeper James Williamson died following his side's 1–1 draw at Rangers on 12 November, 1921.

Port Vale defender Tom Butler died of tetanus when complications set in after he broke his arm in a 1923 game against Clapton Orient.

Bury full back Sam Wynne collapsed shortly before half time whilst taking a free kick against Sheffield United in a First Division game at Bramall Lane on 30 April, 1927. He died in the dressing room, his death blamed on pneumonia.

Goalkeeper John Thomson initially turned down a move to Celtic, because of a premonition his mother had – in a dream she saw him seriously injured whilst playing for the Glasgow club. But by 1931, at the age of 23, Thomson had joined Celtic – only to die at Ibrox Park during a game against Rangers, when he collided with their forward Sam English. The match was played on 5 September, 1931. Thomson dived at the feet of the oncoming English. His skull, later found to be thinner than normal, fractured on impact with the striker's knee.

Thomson died in hospital that evening, having never regained consciousness. Twenty thousand people gathered at Queen Street Station when a funeral train left for his home town of Cardenden in Fife.

On 1 December, 1934 Gillingham striker Sim Raleigh suffered a mid-air collision with Brighton defender Paul Mooney, but after smelling-salt treatment continued to play, only to collapse during the second half. He was taken to hospital, where he died later that evening.

Sunderland goalkeeper James Horatio Thorpe was diabetic. The player, aged 22, was between the sticks on 1 February, 1936, when Chelsea were the visitors for a top of the table clash. It was a physically robust game and Thorpe was injured during a goalmouth mêlée as he clung determinedly on to the ball, but refused attention and played on. When the Sunderland players reported for training on Wednesday, 5 February, it was to be greeted by the news that Thorpe had died in hospital early that morning.

The report of the Coroner's inquest criticised the referee for not taking better control of the match and suggested that 'the violence of the play itself triggered off the diabetic coma which led quickly to the young man's death', wrote Roger Hutchinson in his club history *Into The Light*. An FA Commission, though, exonerated the ref, and the game of football itself. The game had finished 3–3, and Thorpe's widow received his posthumously-awarded championship medal.

Two players were struck by lightning and killed during an Army Cup Final replay at Aldershot in 1948. The referee was also hit, but survived.

During a February 1967 FA Amateur Cup Fourth round game between Highgate United and Enfield, several players were struck by lightning and one of them, United defender Tommy Allden, 23, subsequently died.

Bradford City boss Grenville Hair collapsed and died during a training session on 7 March, 1968.

Tranmere player turned assistant manager Eddie Robertson collapsed and died during a December 1981 training session at West Kirby beach, aged 46 – and was commemorated via a Supporters' Association Players' Player trophy . . . In 1934 the same club had suffered a similar loss when prolific scorer Bert Whitehouse, who had hit 35 goals in 90 games, collapsed and died after training at Prenton Park.

Former Everton manager Harry Catterick died at Goodison Park after an FA Cup quarter final game against Ipswich in March 1985.

One of football's, and definitely Everton's, greatest goalscorers, Dixie Dean, who also played for Tranmere and Notts County, and scored 60 goals in 39 league games for the Toffee men in one season, died at Goodison Park with a minute remaining in the 1980 Merseyside derby with Liverpool.

Scotland boss Jock Stein collapsed at a World Cup qualifier against Wales in September, 1985. Stein, 62, suffered a heart attack as his side battled to equalise, which they later did, to guarantee qualification for the final stages. Stein died the same evening.

Malaga keeper Jose Gallardo collided with another player during a Spanish Second Division game against Vigo on 21 December, 1986, receiving a blow to the head and sustaining the brain haemorrhage from which he died on 15 January, 1987.

Twelve fans were trampled to death in Lagos, Nigeria, and a player died on the field during the 12 August, 1989 World Cup qualifier between Nigeria and Angola.

Goalkeeper Vijendra Singh of the Iqram Institute club in Ghaziabad, India, was killed when a fight broke out after a 1991 semi final against the Times Institute.

Five players were charged with murder following a 1991 game in Swaziland during which an opponent was clubbed to death during a game.

Sudanese newspaper *Alwan* reported in November 1996 that Adel Moustafa, a linesman at a village match at Hasasheisa, one hundred miles from Khartoum, died after being attacked by the disgruntled goalkeeper of a team whose goal he had disallowed.

All eleven members of one team taking part in a match in Eastern Kasai, a south central province of the Democratic Republic of the Congo, in October 1998 were struck by lightning and killed, whilst the away team, from Basangana, remained untouched, reported Associated Press. Suspicions of witchcraft were raised, with Kinshasa paper *L'Avenir* reporting that 'the exact nature of the lightning has divided the population in this region, known for its use of fetishes in

football.' The match was between the home side of Bena Tshadi and Basangana, with AP confirming that the home club suffered the fatalities.

Former Welsh international Robbie James collapsed and died in February 1998 whilst playing for Llanelli, the club he was managing. He was only just in his forties.

A riot broke out following a disputed goal awarded in a South African match held in February 1999. Captain of the Hartbeesfontein Wallabies, Isaac Mkhwetha, left the field – 110 miles west of Johannesburg – to grab a knife. He then lunged with it at referee Lebogang Petrus Mokgethi, who shot him dead with a 9mm pistol which he had just retrieved from a friend amongst the 600 spectators at the game – which was described by a South African spokesman as an unofficial 'gambling game' played for high stakes.

Zambian referee Stephen Longu died from injuries inflicted by enraged supporters of Premier Division club Green Buffaloes in July 1999. Longu was attacked after the team's 1–0 defeat by Kabwe Warriors.

Twenty-seven-year-old Prodromos Papadopoulos scored his sixteenth goal of the season for Greek Fourth Division leaders Patraikos in a 3–1 home win on 11 March, 2000, but died later that day from a heart attack brought on by diabetes which, it transpired, he had kept hidden from club officials who might otherwise have banned him from playing.

Forty-year-old Nick Hinchcliffe from Chudderton, Greater

Manchester, turned out for his first game for two years for his local pub side in June 2000 and scored a match-winning penalty in the closing minutes. Sadly, Nick suffered a heart attack after the game and died in hospital.

Twenty-four-year-old striker Hocine Gacemi died in a Paris hospital after being injured during an Algerian League match, playing for JS Kabylie against USM Annabe, reported *World Soccer*, in June 2000. Gacemi suffered brain damage in a collision. He had been the leading scorer in the League at the time.

Playing for Dinamo Bucharest on 5 October, 2000, international Catalin Haldan, 24, collapsed during the game and died on his way to hospital. He became the fourth player to die suddenly in Romania in the previous two years. A subsequent investigation ruled out suggestions that he had been taking performance-enhancing drugs.

Former Arsenal winger George Armstrong, part of the 1971 League and Cup double side, who made 621 first team appearances for them in fifteen years, collapsed and died on the club's Hertfordshire training field on 1 November, 2000. He was 56.

Referee John Richardson, 50, died of a heart attack whilst officiating at a schoolboy match between Merseyside and Cheshire Under 16s in November 2000.

Jamaican international Steve Malcolm was still wearing his shirt after a game against Bulgaria in Kingston on 28 January, 2001, when he was killed in a car crash near Montego Bay.

Nicknamed Shorty, the 30-year-old had won 76 caps.

DISASTERS

The first of 161 football-related deaths in Argentina, up to September 2000, took place in 1939; and the total included 74 crushed in a major disaster at the River Plate Stadium in 1968, when visiting fans tried to flee the ground after police used teargas.

Forty-one people were killed in 1967 during a Turkish League match when a disallowed goal sparked a riot.

Eighteen fans were killed in November 1982 when a wall collapsed during a match between Tolima, and Deportivo Cali in Ibague, Colombia.

Three hundred and forty were crushed to death in Moscow in July 1982 during a Spartak v Haarlem UEFA Cup tie in Lenin Stadium.

DOG

When Bridge Warriors' manager Alec Watson's black labrador Ozzie died, players wore armbands and held a minute's silence in their dressing room, in memory of the dog, who always attended their matches. The referee refused to sanction a minute's silence on the pitch for the Wiltshire side's mutt in October 2000, but Watson, 53, said, 'Ozzie was a dog in a million. He was the club mascot since 1984.'

In November 1920 Manchester City's Main Stand burnt down. All the club's records were destroyed in the blaze as, sadly, was the club's much loved watchdog, Nell.

Kent side Jordan Rangers wore black armbands in January 2000 after the manager's dog Barney, who attended all their matches, passed away.

When Carlos Bianchi, an Argentinian of Italian descent, won the Argentinian League title with Boca Juniors in a 1–0 victory over Estudiantes, which also clinched the treble for his side in December 2000, he announced: 'It may seem a bit selfish, but I want to dedicate this to my dog who died two days ago.'

Players wore black armbands and held a minute's silence before the Berkeley Arms FC match in Bognor in February 1999, in honour of player Mark Harnett's 13-year-old Jack Russell, George, who died of a stroke.

DOLPHIN

A Dutch woman was killed by a football-playing dolphin in July 1996. The 64-year-old had visited a fun park in Harderwijk, Holland, and watched the dolphin balance a football on his nose then flip it into the crowd – where it hit her on the head and caused her to slip and fall down a flight of steps to her death.

DOUBLE DEATH

Tragedy overtook Nicol Smith of Rangers in 1904, when he

contracted enteric fever. His wife also caught the disease whilst nursing him, and she died. The club arranged a benefit match for him against Queens Park, attended by 10,000, but on the day of the match, 5 January, 1905, Smith suffered a relapse and died two days later, leaving five orphaned children.

DREADLOCKS

Danny Cadamarteri, then of Everton, had his trademark dreadlocks shaved off to make a gesture to mark the death of his father: 'My dad died of cancer,' he told *The Express* in February 2000, 'I just felt I had to do something. I went into the hairdresser and told them to shave the lot off. There were 40 locks, so I bought 40 Everton shirts and had them each framed with a lock and a signature, and then auctioned them off. It raised over five grand for cancer research.'

DROWNED

Peter Campbell, an original player for Rangers when the club was formed, lost his life in 1883 when the steamer on which he was chief engineer sank in the Bay of Biscay.

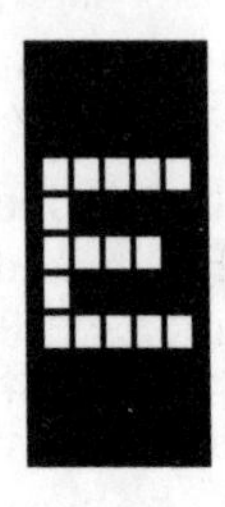

EARTHQUAKE

Two new Argentinian signings for Colombian club Deportivo Quindio, Ruben Bihurriet and Diego Montenegro, were killed in early 1999 when the town of Armenia was wrecked by an earthquake.

END OF THE LINE . . . SMAN

Colombian linesman – or referee, depending on which account you accept – Daniel, or Alvaro, Ortega was murdered by two gunmen in November 1989 after upsetting the crowd for apparently favouring American De Cali in a game against Independiente Medellin, or for officiating the game too impartially. The rumoured reason was that a drugs gang had placed a large bet on an outcome other than that permitted by Sr Ortega. The Colombian League was suspended and the League title withheld. No one was ever convicted of the murder. In 1990 the group Cleansers of Colombian Football carried out six killings.

ETERNAL SLUMBER

Robert Bradley, 27, played for Carlisle in a game at Chester on 17 February, 1934 – and died overnight in his sleep.

EVERYONE KNOWS IT'S . . .

Windy weather at Chelsea home matches activates the weather-vane above the East Stand – which was erected in memory of former international striker George 'Gatling Gun' Hilsdon, who died in 1941 aged 56, having been gassed at Arras during the war.

EXAGGERATION

Legendary Spanish goalkeeper of the 1920s, Ricardo Zamora, who played for both Barcelona and Real Madrid, was reported to have been shot dead during the Spanish Civil War by newspaper *ABC*, but survived to tell the tale, although he was arrested and threatened with execution. He stayed alive by playing football with his captors.

EXECUTION

A player banned from a 1990 game in Beirut shot his coach dead and was then executed by local militia, reported the *Sportspages Almanac 1991*.

Brighton's original home, the Goldstone ground, was the site of two public executions in 1793 when two robbers were hung, then in 1795 witnessed the firing-squad demise of two soldiers charged with desertion.

EXTRA TIME

Fifty-four-year-old Roy Race, a well known striker, was killed in a helicopter crash in March 1993 – but not for long! Race, formerly a player for Melchester Rovers, was re-born several months later and became manager of a top Italian side. The fact that Race was the eponymous Roy of the Rovers may have had something to do with his miraculous reincarnation.

Many football fans claim to die a thousand deaths whilst watching their favourite side: Celtic supporter Harry Moin literally died during a match – and lived to tell the tale. Forty-two-year-old Harry suffered a heart attack at a game and ended up technically dead for three minutes before being revived. He was later fitted with a defribilator in his chest: 'If I do have another arrest this little gadget will shock me back to life,' he said in October 1999.

FAN-TASTIC GESTURE

The whole Real Sociedad side wore the name A Zabaleta on their shirts in a 1998–99 Primera Liga match against Real Madrid as a mark of respect to the fan of that name stabbed to death by Madrid hooligans before a Cup match between the sides.

FATAL FOOTBALLS

When the 8th Battalion The East Surrey Regiment attacked Prussian Guards on the Somme on 1 July, 1916, Captain W.P. Nevill produced four footballs – which they dribbled and kicked in front of them as they advanced across no-man's land. Nevill himself was killed in the attack, but the ridge was captured. *The Daily Mail* recorded the event in poignant verse: 'On through the hail of slaughter, Where gallant comrades fall, Where blood is poured like water, They drive the trickling ball. The fear of death before them Is but an empty name True to the land that bore them The Surreys play the game.' One of the footballs was later sent back to Kingston Barracks to be retained as a regimental trophy.

FATALITIES

A September 1998 survey by Middlesex University revealed swimming to be the most dangerous sport in 1988–92 in England and Wales, producing 191 fatalities. Football was eighth on the list, with fourteen.

FATAL PHOTO

A man working for the undertaker carrying out Sir Matt Busby's 1994 funeral took photographs of the Man U boss lying in his coffin and tried to sell them to the highest newspaper bid. He was 'shopped' and arrested.

FERRET

Wealden Wanderers players wore black armbands during a match in January 2001 following the death of their mascot Eddie – a ferret. 'He came to all our games and brought us luck,' declared skipper Leon Walsh, 27, from Tonbridge, Kent.

FINAL TREAT

Soccer-crazy Fred Swann's family were convinced that the lifelong Millwall fan would want to be at Wembley Stadium when the club finally made it for the Auto Windscreen Shield Final against Wigan in 1999. So they bought Fred a ticket – even though he had been dead for five years. The ticket was placed on an empty seat during the match, which Millwall lost to a last-minute Wigan goal.

FIRST FOOTBALL FATALITY?

'The first recorded death in a football match came in 1892, when St Mirren player James Dunlop died of tetanus after suffering a cut on the pitch during a game,' according to Jim Drewett and Alex Leith, authors of *The Virgin Book of Football Records*. The authors reckon 'one of the nastiest ever football deaths' was suffered by Thomas Grice of Aston, in 1897, who was killed on the pitch when he stumbled to the ground and his belt buckle 'punctured his stomach'. But I have discovered a number of incidents which cast doubt on the former assertion.

In March 1878 one William Bradshaw, who had been charged with the manslaughter of Herbert Dockerty during a football match between Ashby de la Zouch and Coalville, was acquitted, despite evidence that he 'jumped in the air and struck him in the stomach with his knee'.

In 1889 former Hibs player Dan Doyle, who had moved to Grimsby Town, accidentally kicked opponent William Cropper of Staveley in the stomach. Cropper, a professional cricketer with Derbyshire, died from his injuries.

On Christmas day of the same year former England international winger, Liverpool and Spurs player Tom Bradshaw, then skipper of Thames Ironworks – who would soon become West Ham – died from injuries sustained in a 1–0 win against Bedminster.

The top side in Scotland in the early days of the organised game of football was Queen's Park and a Minute of the club's committee meeting of 28 November, 1890, said: 'Reference was made to the sad death of Mr H. M. Walters, resulting from an accident on the football field.' The club sent a wreath and letter of condolence to the funeral.

There is, though, competition for the title of First Football Fatality. In Derby there was an old-established mass game of football as far back as the early eighteenth century and it is recorded that around 1850 a participant was drowned in the Derwent during the course of one of these

annual matches. Even further back, on Trinity Sunday, 1280, at Ulgham, Northumberland, it is recorded in a 1916 work, *The Calendar of Inquisitions*, 'One Henry, son of William de Ellington was playing at football with a large number of friends. In the course of play he ran against David le Keu, who was wearing a knife. The unfortunate Henry impaled himself on the knife and subsequently died.' This type of thing seems to have been something of an occupational hazard of the age as there is a 1321 record of a special Papal dispensation of blame for a certain William de Spalding following this incident: 'During the game at ball as he kicked the ball, a lay friend of his, also called William, ran against him and wounded himself on a sheathed knife carried by the canon so severely that he died within six days.'

On 25 March, 1303, according to *Records Of Medieval Oxford*, H. E. Salter's seminal work of 1912, 'An Oxford student, Adam of Salisbury, was performing his football skills in the High Street. He was attacked by a gang of Irish students, and mortally wounded.' In 1322 a Gilbertine Canon of Shouldham, Norfolk, William de Spalding, accidentally killed a friend in the course of a football game, we are told by Percy Young in his *A History of British Football*. Even worse, in 1321 a servant at the Cistercian Abbey of Vale Royal was murdered by two brothers named Oldyngton, who used the head of the deceased as a football. Ancient Coroner's Court records of 1583 report: 'Roger Ludforde, of South Mimms, ran towards the ball with the intention to kick it, whereupon Nicholas Martyn with the fore-part of his right arm and Richard Torvey with the fore-part of his left arm struck Roger Ludforde on the fore-part of the body under the breast, giving him a mortal blow and concussion of which he died within a quarter of an hour, and that Nicholas and Richard in this manner feloniously slew the said Roger.'

FISHY

Fans threw dead fish on to the pitch during Hungary's February 2000 home game with Australia, in protest at a cyanide spill by a part-Aussie owned company which allegedly killed wildlife in two Danube tributaries.

Flooding at Notts County's Meadow Lane pitch in December 2000 left the playing surface covered with dead fish.

FLARE UP

Red Star fan Aleksander Radovic became the first person killed by hooliganism in the history of Yugoslav football when, in December 1999, he was hit by a flare thrown during a match against Partizan, in Belgrade.

FUNERAL ARRANGEMENTS

When Barnsley were due to play Newcastle in a vital FA Cup match during the 1945–6 season, management at the local collieries feared mass absenteeism. One put up a notice: 'Will those whose relatives are to be buried on that day please apply by Tuesday for permission to attend.'

'The funeral of the future could include pop songs and coffins draped with football strips,' predicted the Co-Operative Funeral Service in a press release on 20 March, 2000. The next month the Manchester based United Norwest Co-Op went a little further: 'Coffins would be in football colours,' said Marketing Manager Phil Lane. 'The funeral procession would go past the ground and you'd have the team's song playing at the service.'

Lifelong Newcastle supporter Cardinal Basil Hulme requested that the *Match of the Day* theme tune should be played at his funeral. Sadly when he died in June 1999, Westminster Abbey failed to agree to his request. However, friends arranged for the music to be played at a memorial service in Newcastle, held on 1 July, 1999.

Given compassionate leave to attend the funeral of a relative, and to miss a League match the week before the FA Cup Final in 1963–64, Preston left half Ian Davidson suddenly found himself dropped from the Final and suspended for two weeks, as the club announced they did not believe his excuse.

Former FA Chief Executive turned Luton Town director, Graham Kelly, revealed in 1999 that his choice for the music to be played at his funeral included England's France "98 theme, 'On Top of the World', and the Animals' 'We Gotta Get Out Of This Place'.

Nottingham Forest supporter Sam Anscombe, 43, who would only drive a red car, was buried wearing a Forest shirt, in a coffin decorated with club colours. All the mourners wore red and white, and sang the club song, 'He's Got The Whole World In His Hands', in February 1998.

Referee Mick Johnston was buried in his black kit together with his whistle and a red card after dying suddenly, aged 40, at Teesside in December 1996.

Liverpool striker Titi Camara hit the only goal of the game at Anfield to beat West Ham in their October 1999

Premiership clash, then revealed that his father had died the previous day. Camara had to miss the funeral but burst into tears after scoring and said, 'That goal was for my father.'

Questions to Bradford City scout Andy Smith about the club's stiffs, as the reserves are known, had a double meaning for the man, who, in the early 2000s, doubled up by running a funeral director's business in Wakefield.

Former Scotland and Everton striker, my namesake, Graeme Sharp, still carries out a certain amount of PR work for his former club: "I've attended a couple of funerals of lads who were lifelong Evertonians. At one, nobody was to wear black, just their Everton strip – even the Liverpudlians. At the other one I went to the guy was buried in a royal blue coffin."

GALLOWS

George Raynor, a Yorkshireman, became manager of Lazio in the mid-1950s and his selection of a goalkeeper resulted in potential execution for the chosen custodian. Writing in his autobiography, *Football Administrator At Large*, Raynor recalled: 'Our goalkeeper had been weak, so I substituted an old man of something like 35 years of age. The newspapers called me crazy and demanded that I resign immediately.' The fans went further and the club director warned Raynor 'that the rabid supporters had set up some gallows and that they would hang him if Lazio lost'. Lazio won that match, but Raynor remained wary of Lazio fans, of which his butcher was a fine example: 'If we lost there would be no deliveries. And if we lost a couple of matches he would leave a small wooden coffin outside the door.'

GARAGE

Vicenza keeper Pierluigi Brivio opened his garage in December 1998 to discover two corpses in a blood-spattered

car. A man had shot his hairdresser lover and then himself, police said.

GHOSTS

The ghost of former manager Herbert Chapman is said to haunt the corridors of Highbury.

In 1996, 23-year-old club barmaid Vicky Lowe asked Reading for permission to bury her dead hamster, Miss Effie, in the goalmouth at their then Elm Park Tilehurst Road end. The hamster was duly interred by groundsman Gordon Neate alongside the ashes of a number of supporters and a past chairman, reported *The Guardian* under the headline 'A Tale of Mice and Men'. Vicky believed that Miss Effie's interment was crucial in the club's battle against relegation that season: 'Her ghost distracted the opposition,' she declared.

Reg Matthews, Derby County keeper of the sixties, refused to cross the threshold of Bisham Abbey when his Brian Clough-bossed side went there for a training stint. He was unnerved by the ghostly vibes he picked up. As was Sheffield Wednesday boss, Peter Shreeve in the nineties – who confirmed the spooky feeling of the place, which is reputedly haunted by the shade of a sixteenth-century mother who cuffed her naughty child round the ear before locking him in a cupboard there, only to find him dead on her return. The Abbey is also reputedly the site of an overspill graveyard for bodies shipped down from London centuries ago.

Sixty-three-year-old Leeds fan Ken Jones was convinced that his car had become haunted by Sir Matt Busby. The L-reg

Ford Mondeo suffered a series of faults whilst being driven to matches at Elland Road, but when mechanics checked it over they could find no fault. Ken sent off for a copy of the car's log book, and discovered that in 1993 it was registered to the ownership of Sir Matt – a year before the United supremo died. 'Sir Matt must be haunting the car,' said Ken in September 2000. 'He must be livid that his motor has ended up in the hands of a Leeds supporter – each time it is repaired it is OK for a while, but it is not long before Sir Matt strikes again.'

Manchester United centre half Charlie Roberts, who died in 1939 aged 56, was known as 'the ghost in boots' because of his habitually pale countenance.

Fred, a supporter who died during a match in the 1960s, is believed to haunt Oldham's Boundary Park's George Hill stand, where cleaners refused to work alone after he was spotted several times.

The ghost of former Hibs' boss of the fifties, Harry Swann, was reportedly seen near the old West Stand – since demolished. It was even claimed that the wee ghoulie would shake hands with people before disappearing.

GRAVE MISTAKE

The first black professional footballer Arthur Wharton, born in Gold Coast – now known as Ghana – who turned out in goal for Sheffield United in Division One in 1895, having begun his paid career at Rotherham in 1889, was buried in a pauper's grave at Edlington, near Doncaster, following his death on 12 October, 1930. In May 1997, thanks to research

by Phil Vasili who wrote a book about Wharton, his resting place was finally marked with a fine headstone carrying a tribute to him which was unveiled at a dignified ceremony. Bafflingly, though, the headstone referred to his date of death as 13 October, 1930.

Cardiff City supporter Grahame Lloyd was researching his book *A Hundred Years of the Bluebirds* when he discovered that the man credited with being the driving force behind founding the club was buried in an unmarked grave. Disabled lithographic artist Walter Bartley Wilson, known as Bart, had died on 19 November, 1954, but was in Western Cemetery, Cardiff, in a plot known only as Plot 246, alongside his wife Sarah. Lloyd discovered that a headstone had been made but never erected, so he organised a rededication service and a new headstone – but the old one was found and restored.

Southampton's new stadium in the St Mary's dockland area of the city is sited on a pre-Christian graveyard.

GRAVE EMPLOYMENT

Former Manchester City winger Mike Summerbee worked at one time as a gravedigger.

GUN

A soccer fan shot dead his son in August 1997 whilst celebrating Turkey's 6–4 World Cup victory over Wales. The father, watching the match on TV in Adana, fired his shotgun in joy at the final whistle, only to hit his 15-year-old son.

Croatian World Cup celebrations following their 1998 victory over Germany included gunshots, one of which killed a 26-year-old woman in Mostar.

After Iraq beat China 1–0 during a 1993 World Cup qualifier, nine people were reported dead and 120 injured from 'rogue gunfire' during celebrations.

HAMMER

Popular KR Reykjavik striker Einar Orn Birgisson, 27, was battered to death with a hammer by his former team mate Atli Helgason, reported the February 2001 edition of *World Soccer*. Helgason apparently confessed to the crime and led police to the body, which was hidden behind lava rocks in Grindavik.

HAMSTER

A pet hamster was killed by an exploding football in August 1998. Southampton student Wayne Beale, 27, said: 'There was a huge bang. Then I found the remnants of the ball and Trevor the Hamster dead in his cage next to it.'

HEADSTONE . . .

The inscription on the headstone of former Norwich centre half turned Class One ref George Miller, who died in December 1931 aged 56, reads: 'When the Great Recorder

comes to write against your name, He'll write not how you won or lost but how you played the game.'

HEDGEHOG

A 14-year-old boy, who could not be named for legal reasons, was sentenced to three months working with animals in January 2001 after being found guilty by Guildford magistrates of kicking a hedgehog to death while whistling the *Match of the Day* theme tune.

HELICOPTER

Multi-millionaire and Chelsea vice-chairman Matthew Harding, the 89th richest man in the country, died in a helicopter crash in Cheshire in October 1996, on the way back from Chelsea's Coca Cola Cup defeat at Bolton.

HIGH COST

The official estimate is that 75 British footballers gave their lives during the Second World War.

HIGH SPIRITS . . .

Spoon bender Uri Geller alarmed officials at Swansea after warning them that their Vetch Field ground was inhabited by 'black spirits'. In an effort to remove the problem, Swansea invited witch doctors the Kenyan Boys who were, in early 2001, touring locally with the Cottle & Austen Circus, to help eliminate the spirits. 'When Uri Geller visited us he said there were black spirits at the club – he even claimed they caused the suicide of one of our players, Tich Evans,

who played here in the 1920s,' revealed Swansea communications manager Peter Owen. At time of writing the efficacy of the Kenyan Boys' 'exorcism' was yet to be established, as the pitch was waterlogged and they couldn't actually get on it.

HOGGING LIMELIGHT

Only one of London's countless number of statues boasts a football – it stands on a marble pedestal in Langham Place near BBC's Broadcasting House and is a bronze memorial to the late Scottish international Quintin Hogg, who played in the first ever match against England in 1870.

HORSING ABOUT

A coal merchant's horse, which died in a 1931 accident during the building of terrace extensions to Highbury was, according to legend, buried under the North Bank stand. When the site was bulldozed in 1992 the horse itself was not discovered although a couple of horseshoes were turned up. Other remains may, though, have been lost amongst the rubble.

IDENTITY

Twenty-two-year-old Brazilian, Gil, was so desperate to play in Europe that he took on the identity of a dead Portuguese named Rodrigues after being given his documents by his agent. He confessed what he had done to a Brazilian Senate commission of inquiry in early 2001, after having spent a season playing for Spanish clubs Hercules and Lorca. 'All this only got out because my agent told the papers following a night of heavy drinking,' said Gil, who returned to Brazil to play for Nautico.

IDOLATRY

Religious leaders accused fans of idolatry following Zambia's defeat by Tunisia in the 1996 African Nations Cup when it emerged that supporters had prayed for victory at the graves of the eighteen members of the Zambian national side killed in a 1993 air crash. Local reports declared: 'A Christian nation like Zambia must recognise God's supremacy in all things, including football.'

IN THE LONG RUN . . .

Former Fulham, Millwall, QPR and Brentford winger Barry Salvage collapsed and died aged 38, whilst on a charity run in Eastbourne in October, 1986.

JEWELLERY JOKE BACKFIRED

Visiting a jewellery shop in Rome in 1977, Lazio player Luciano Re Cecconi decided to play a joke on the owner, waggling his hands in his pockets and ordering: 'Raise your hands'. The proprietor, Bruno Tabocchini, had been robbed before and had bought a pistol to protect himself, which he now produced and fired at Cecconi. Initially arrested for manslaughter, the jeweller was later freed when a court found that he had no case to answer.

JINXED FIXTURE

On two occasions, matches between two of South Africa's top clubs, Orlando Pirates and Kaiser Chiefs, have resulted in the deaths of over 40 people. In 1991 the two sides met in a pre-season friendly in the mining town of Orkney and 41 died in a stampede. In April 2001 at least 43 perished in similar scenes at Johannesburg's Ellis Park Stadium.

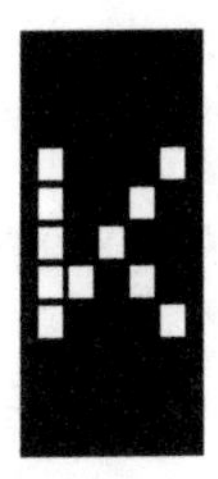

KILLING FIELD

Chile had no problem taking the lead against USSR in their November 1973 World Cup qualifying match – as the Soviets had failed to turn up, in protest at the match being played in Santiago's Estadio Nacional which had been used as a detention centre for dissidents during a military crackdown in which firing squads had killed many. 'Soviet sportsmen cannot play on a ground stained with the blood of Chilean patriots,' said Soviet Football Federation chief Valentin Granatkin.

KILLING KIEV

In August 1942, after Hitler had invaded the Soviet Union, a football match took place in Ukraine between a German Luftwaffe side and a team of impoverished Kievans from a local bakery, FC Start. The Start team included members of the Dynamo Kiev side, which had been officially disbanded, and their local rivals Lokomotiv. They played a series of games, beating the Luftwaffe side once, but then taking them on again in a game before which a senior Nazi demanded that they shout 'Heil Hitler!'. They refused.

After the game, which FC Start won, despite an SS officer refereeing, the players were banished to Siretz concentration camp where four of them were executed, including keeper Nikolai Trusevich, who died 'on his feet wearing his familiar black and red jersey.' A three-metre-high monument stands outside the Dynamo stadium in memory of the 'death match'. The full story is told in Andy Dougan's *Dynamo: Defending the Honour of Kiev*.

KRAYZY

Kirkby, Nottinghamshire, side Ashfield 95 appointed jailed murderer Reggie Kray club president in February 1997 – after he agreed to donate £1,000 towards their hunt for a better ground.

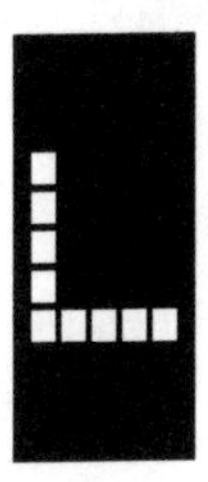

LAST WORDS

Lifelong Sunderland fan Ron Hutcheon, 71, was on the way home from his side's December 2000 victory over Newcastle when he suffered a massive heart attack. As he collapsed he uttered his final words . . . '2–1' . . . the score of the match. His widow, speaking from their red and white painted house, said, 'It is a comfort to know he died happy.'

LEUKAEMIA

Medical research in Italy, published in mid-2000 revealed an incidence of leukaemia amongst footballers 35 times higher than that of the general population. In all, 165 premature deaths of former footballers were investigated and the inference was that the prolonged misuse of anabolic steroids could be responsible, as it is believed to provoke the condition.

LUCKLESS LIPSHAM

Herbert Lipsham of Crewe, Sheffield United and Fulham, who won full international honours for England in 1902, emigrated to Canada, where he first lost a hand in a timber-yard accident and then died in a 1954 train crash.

LUCKY COFFIN

On the eve of the 1887 Scottish Cup Final Hibs player Phil Clarke received a gift from Glasgow's Irish community – a miniature black coffin with a cross and harp on the lid and a skeleton inside – allegedly for GOOD luck! It worked – Clarke scored in a 2–1 win over Dumbarton.

MAD HATTER?

When Freddie Pentland died in Dorset in 1962, his demise was commemorated at the San Mames ground of Athletic Bilbao. A high-kicking dance celebrated the eccentric Englishman who coached the side in the 1920s, wearing a bowler hat which would be ritually trashed by the players whenever they won a match. A small memorial was also put in place.

MANSLAUGHTER . . .

Alex Young scored the winning goal in the 1906 FA Cup Final for Everton against Newcastle. He later played for Spurs and Manchester City before emigrating in 1914 to Australia, where he was charged the following year with the murder of his brother. Evidence that he had been prone to bouts of temporary insanity was given by the English football authorities, and in June 1916 he was found guilty of manslaughter and sentenced to three years in jail. Years later he returned to his native Scotland, where he died in 1959.

A match played in Leicester in 1898 ended in tragedy as John Briggs of Aylestone died from serious internal injuries sustained during a match against Enderby, whose Henry Moore was found guilty of manslaughter, following evidence heard at Leicester Assizes that 'Moore jumped with his knees up against Briggs' back and threw him violently forward against the knees of the goalkeeper.' Oddly, a witness called Veasey, who played in that game and gave evidence against Moore, was himself killed several days later during a match.

Referee William Ernest Williams was killed in 1912 by a player named Hansford, after a Welsh football match between Wattstown and Aberaman Athletic. Hansford was jailed for manslaughter.

Wolves midfielder James Kelly was jailed for five years in February 1996, after admitting to the manslaughter of a 26-year-old man.

Best pals James Cassidy, a Celtic supporter, and John Hutchinson, a Rangers fan, came to blows after Celtic won an old firm derby 1–0. In the ensuing fight, Cassidy, using a knife, assaulted and killed his friend. In November 1999 Cassidy admitted manslaughter and was jailed for four years.

Pelé's son, Edinho, a goalkeeper, was found guilty of manslaughter in late 1999 after being accused of racing another car through Santos and causing the death of an elderly motorcyclist, who was struck by the other car. Edinho was given a 'semi-open' six-year sentence.

MEMORIAL

Liverpool erected a memorial to those who died in the Hillsborough tragedy alongside the Shankly Gates, themselves a permanent memorial to manager Bill Shankly – a bronze statue by sculptor Tom Kelly in his honour was unveiled in 1998 by his widow Nessie.

In 1922 one of the legendary figures of Spanish football, prolific Athletic Bilbao striker Pichichi Moreno, died of typhus aged just 29. He was 'mourned in the manner of Rudolf Valentino' and to this day opposing teams lay bouquets of flowers at the base of the bust unveiled in his honour.

A statue in honour of former player and manager Billy Bremner was erected outside Elland Road following his 1997 death from a heart attack, aged 54.

Woodend Rangers and Wibsey prepared to do battle for the Basil Smith Memorial Trophy of the Grattan League in Bradford, in 1997, only for a stray warm-up shot to smash the trophy, which Mr Smith's widow, Betty, had been invited along to present.

MISTAKEN IDENTITY

When Manchester City, then English champions, were on tour in the USA in the summer of 1968, they had with them defender Bobby Kennedy. During the tour, manager Joe Mercer imposed a strict 10pm curfew on the players, so he and chairman Albert Alexander were stunned to hear on the 11pm TV news that Bobby Kennedy had been shot. Unaware

of the politician of the same name, Alexander reportedly said: 'It's his own fault for being out so late.'

MONUMENTAL MARTYR

The death at the age of 27 of Romanian Second Division striker, Florin Piturca after he returned home from a December 1978 match for Drobeta Turnu Severin, affected his father Maximilian greatly.

There were rumours that Piturca's death occurred after he and other players were given drugs in their half time tea.

Maximilian, a cobbler, built a tomb in honour of his son and stayed there every night – sleeping there after doing a day's work.

Then he commissioned a sculptor to make a life-size bronze statue in his son's image.

In March 1989 Zoe Ceausescu visited the cemetery and decided that the tomb and its accompanying memorial should be removed. She ordered bulldozers in the carry out the work.

Maximilian was inside the tomb when it was destroyed – as he came out he reportedly swore a curse on Ceausescu's family – "In a year I will be back and you will be dead" he cried.

Within a year the ruling Ceausescus were overthrown and executed – the Piturca tomb was rebuilt and Maximilian resumed his nightly vigil there, remaining even when struck down from a heart attack which eventually led to his death in 1994.

Shortly before he died he told his wife Vasilica: "I am very happy that soon I will see my son again."

MURDER

Aston Villa defender Thomas Ball became the only British

professional player to be murdered when, on 10 November, 1923, a day after playing for Villa in their 1–0 win over Notts County at Meadow Lane, he was shot dead by neighbour George Stagg, following an argument about Ball's dog and chickens straying on to Stagg's land. Stagg was found guilty and sentenced to hang, but was reprieved and given life imprisonment.

George and Ted Robledo were sons of an English mother and Chilean father, who played for Barnsley and Newcastle, both appearing for the latter in their 1952 FA Cup Final victory over Arsenal. Both also represented Chile in the World Cup. Ted may have been murdered in 1970. Returning from England to the Persian Gulf, where he was working, on the *Al Sahn*, sailing out of Dubai, Ted went missing. The ship's captain was charged with murder, but acquitted. Ted's body was never found.

Retired Yugoslav policeman Marinko Janevski strangled his wife when she turned off their TV during a football match. During his 1982 trial he pleaded that her actions were 'an extreme provocation' and claimed in his defence that 'I always get excited when watching football.' He was found guilty by the Belgrade jury.

A documentary made about Lutz Eigendorf, capped six times for East Germany, alleged that his 1983 death in a car crash was actually a murder organised by the Stasi secret police. Eigendorf defected in 1979, seeking political asylum when Dynamo Berlin played in a match in West Germany. The film alleged that Eigendorf, a reported non-drinker who was nonetheless found to have a large amount of alcohol in his blood following the crash, was killed for 'deserting the Republic'.

Emilio Guruceta, the referee accused of accepting a bribe to ensure that Anderlecht beat Nottingham Forest to reach the Final of the UEFA Cup in 1984, may have been murdered, suggests author Phil Ball in his 2001 book, *Morbo: The Story of Spanish Football*. Ball says that he was staying in a San Sebastian hotel when, during a power cut, a man who had once been a linesman for Guruceta, who had died in a 1987 car crash, 'made a cryptic comment implying that Guruceta was murdered.'

Chinese teenager Xia Qian Li murdered his father in June 1990, after being refused permission to watch the World Cup opening ceremony.

As work to redevelop Blackburn's Ewood Park ground in 1994 continued, workers digging the foundations for a new boundary wall discovered what they thought was an old football. Closer inspection revealed that it was the severed head of a woman. Further investigations produced a woman's dismembered torso wrapped in polythene. Forensic scientists identified the victim, and her Accrington-based murderer was subsequently brought to book.

Ten days after scoring an own goal during Colombia's 1994 World Cup game against USA, which they lost 2–1, defender Andres Escobar was shot dead for reasons which have never become completely clear. Rumours of hit-men, gambling coups and drug dealers have circulated. Humberto Munoz Castro confessed to his murder and was sentenced to 43 years in prison.

Larisa Nechayeva, business manager of Spartak Moscow, was gunned down in her car in a suspected Russian Mafia contract killing in June 1997.

Dutch star Clarence Seedorf found himself involved in a murder enquiry after a night out with Cheryl Harkisoen, alias Miss Ajax, ended in tragedy when a knife attacker killed first her, then himself.

A Romanian soccer fan watching his country play Colombia during the 1998 World Cup murdered his wife when she switched the TV off at half-time. Sixty-one-year-old Pavel Weber beat Maria, 57, to death in the town of Satu Mare – and then went off to a local bar to watch the second half.

A German football supporter killed his best friend in September 2000 because he was so slow getting ready that they missed their team's first goal during the Second Division game between Arminia Bielefeld and Rot-Weiss Oberhausen. The pair argued, then fought. The murderer confessed to the police.

A Barcelona supporter was shot dead by a Real Madrid fan following Barcelona's Championship League match in Leeds in October 2000. The 57-year-old Real fan, from Villa Chinchillar in south eastern Spain, celebrated what he thought was Barcelona's defeat by letting off fireworks. His 38-year-old neighbour, a Barcelona-supporting baker, was unhappy and the two became involved in an argument which resulted in the Real fan bringing out a hunting rifle and shooting the other. Barcelona equalised in injury time.

Murderers are amongst the Durham Prison workers who make up to 750 goal nets a year, which are sold to Premier League and other clubs, including Leeds and Sunderland. They cost up to £200 a time and were the first in the world to be personalised with a team logo.

Manchester United fan Chen Jiong was sentenced to death in September 2001 for murdering his Shanghai rubber factory boss who refused him time off to watch a televised United match.

MURDER

Killer Stephen Craven, who claimed an order barring him from watching Newcastle whilst on parole was a breach of his human rights, lost his legal battle to overturn the ban in September 2001. Justice Stanley Burton said: 'His inability to watch Newcastle United is, in the scheme of things, insufficient weight to lead me to reject the exclusion zone.'

MYSTERY

Mickey Hamill, a Manchester United inside forward converted to wing half by Manchester City, in which position he won seven Irish caps, 'suffered a tragic end when his body was fished out of a canal in mysterious circumstances, in July 1943' at the age of 48, records the *Maine Road Encyclopaedia* by Ian Penney.

NAME GAME

One wonders whether the parents of Blackburn centre half Robert Ireland Pryde, who died aged 85 in June 1998, stopped to think what initials they had lumbered him with.

Blue Murder was the name of a now-defunct Manchester City fanzine.

West Brom boasted a club secretary called Frank Heaven during the late 1890s. Steve Death turned out for both West Ham and Reading; Chester put Geoff Coffin on the teamsheet, while Mark Graves was a Plymouth player and John Skull a Swindon man. Andy Graver played for Newcastle, Lincoln, Leicester and Stoke in the 1950s.

Real Madrid and Spain striker Emilio Butragueno was nicknamed the Vulture.

In 1928 Sunderland boasted a left winger named Billy Death.

NARROW ESCAPE

Cricket commentator John Arlott, who died aged 77 in December 1991, had been a football writer in the 1950s for *The Manchester Guardian* and only the last-minute availability of writer Dan Davies saved him from the 1958 Munich air crash.

After hurting his head as a result of a tackle during a match for Selkirk United in Nailsea, Colin Pharo, 28, went for an X-ray, which revealed he had a potentially fatal tumour the size of a grapefruit growing on his brain. 'If I hadn't made that tackle I dread to think what would have happened – doctors told me the tumour would have gone unnoticed and probably killed me,' said Colin in September 2000.

Schoolboy footballer Joe Edwards, 18, effectively 'died' during a match, only to live to tell the tale. Joe, of Kingsteignton, Devon, collapsed during the March 2000 game in which he was turning out for Teign School, but received immediate first aid and was believed to be the first person ever to survive a brugada attack – one of the world's rarest heart conditions.

OBITUARY

Scotland manager Craig Brown appeared as the main guest on BBC Radio 5 Live's *Live Obituary Show* in August 2000, discussing how his life would ultimately be remembered.

When Ghanaian football chairman and administrator Kojo Nunoo died in July 2000, the official obituary issued on his behalf by governing body GHALCA made intriguing reading:

> To everything there is a season, and a time for every purpose under the heaven. A time to be born, and a time to die, so says the good book. It is a known fact that from the very day we were born that we shall be bidding farewell to this world but the pains associated with the loss of a loved one like Mr Kojo Nunoo and the timing of the departure make it difficult for one to come to terms with death.
>
> Mr Kojo Nunoo, who we all knew as Uncle Kojo, fell within the rare species of 'perfect football

administrators', and did more than his fair share to uplift the game of football. Uncle Kojo's humility, respect and leadership quantities were beyond description. Since he joined GHALCA – then known as OGLCA – from his days with Hasaacas, through Kotoko and then to Goldfields, he never refused any assignment given him whether big or small. He was one of the few club chairmen we can, without any difficulty, press our hands on as a role model.

His infectious smile was always available to calm nerves during heated debates, which are very common within football circles. It is going to be a very difficult task finding a replacement for a thoroughbred football administrator cast in the mould of Uncle Kojo, but we take consolation from the fact that the Lord has prepared a better place for him in his bosom.

Uncle Kojo, you were the finest.

Fare thee well.'

PENALTY SHOOT OUTS

Penalty shoot-outs can kill fans, claimed researchers at the University Medical Centre, Utrecht, Holland, in December 2000 after looking at deaths on the day in June 1996 when Holland lost on penalties to France, thus going out of the tournament. They compared death rates with the five days before and after the match, and compared the same period with other years. Deaths from heart attacks or strokes in men, but not women, rose 50 per cent. In the *British Medical Journal*, Professor Diedrick Grobbee said that unusual mental or emotional stress and high alcohol consumption are recognised triggers for strokes and heart attacks.

Goalkeeper Conio Vazques, 23, saved three of five penalties in a March 1996 shoot-out in Bogota, Colombia, only to be shot dead by a local drugs baron, who had reportedly bet heavily on the opposing team.

PIGEON

Striker Duncan Ferguson is a keen pigeon fancier, who races his birds and is prepared to go to great lengths to win races, claimed the *Daily Star* in December 1998, accusing him of shooting dead one of his pigeons. Ferguson's bird had returned in time to win a race, but perched on a roof and wouldn't budge. The striker needed to clock the bird's leg tag through a machine to confirm its time of arrival, 'so he shot it and ran its corpse through the clocking machine.'

PIG SICK

The Observer newspaper told the story in January 2000 of Indonesian star player, Mistar, aged 25, 'killed by a herd of pigs that invaded his team's training pitch before a Cup fixture.'

PLANE CRASH

Seventeen players from Soviet club Tashkent were killed in a 1979 plane crash whilst travelling to a League match.

Forty-three players and officials of Alianza, from Lima, Peru, died in a December 1987 plane crash.

Eighteen members of the Zambian national team were killed in April 1993 when their plane crashed after a refuelling stop en route to a World Cup qualifier against Senegal.

PNEU BOY

Turning out for his side Loughborough Town in an 1896 match against Newton Heath – later to become Man U – James Logan, 25, discovered the team was a kit short, so had to wear his own clothes during the 90-minute game, played in a downpour. As a result he contracted pneumonia and died on 25 May, 1896.

John Haworth, Burnley manager since 1910, caught pneumonia and died while still in office in 1924.

POOLED

Poverty-stricken 46-year-old Susan Nairn of Widnes won £560,000 on the Littlewoods football pools in May 1999 – but collapsed and died hours before the presentation.

POSTHUMOUS BAN

An Italian amateur footballer was banned for one match – nine days after being shot dead. Luigi Coluccio, 23, was killed on 1 November, 1995, by a gunman in Gioisa Jonica, southern Italy, two days after he had been sent off whilst playing in the Calabrian League for his local side. He was duly suspended, despite no longer being alive. League President Nino Cosentino explained that 'the posthumous suspension was unavoidable, since the referee's report was submitted before the shooting'. It could also count, he said, at the end of the season, when fair play awards were decided.

PROGRAMME

A programme for the Manchester United game against Wolves, scheduled for February 1958 but called off because of the Munich air disaster, was sold at auction for £4,830 in April 2000.

QUOTES . . .

Asked 'How would you like to die?', Nottingham Forest club captain Chris Bart-Williams replied: 'Saving someone else's life.'

'The secret of life is to wake up the next morning' according to then manager of Notts County, Jimmy Sirrel.

'In Italy we say that leaving is a little bit like dying, but change is a little like being born' . . . Gianluca Vialli.

'From the bloke's expression, you would have thought I had killed his parents'. Marseille player Djamel Belmadi, who in March 2001 threw his boots at an abusive fan.

'God can tell Heaven's XI to start getting changed, the captain has arrived.' *The Sun* after Bobby Moore's death.

Confirming that Oxford United were the first side of the 2000–1 season to be relegated, on 7 April, 2001, Richard Littlejohn, host of the popular Radio 5 Live *606* phone-in programme, informed their supporters: 'We're running an alternative service to the Samaritans tonight – if you feel like killing yourself, give us a ring and we'll tell you how to do it.'

'Your clients, Mr Thorley, pervade every moment of a fan's life. Do they do gravestones with Arsenal on?' . . . 53-year-old judge Mr Justice Laddie to Arsenal QC Simon Thorley, during a 2001 case involving the alleged infringement of copyright of official club merchandise.

'I want the fans to know that before I finish my career we are going to win something. Otherwise I'll kill myself' . . . West Ham's Paolo di Canio, quoted in *The Sun* in January, 2001.

'If the teams are supported by people who bring about death, football doesn't make sense any more.' So reflected a Bulgarian Football Federation spokesman after 30-year-old Mladen Mladenov died after the Levski Sofia v CSKA Sofia derby, when a firecracker was thrown at him.

'I will die a Catholic. I will die an Arsenal fan and I will die a Tory' . . . threat, promise or prediction in April 2001 by former MP and Governor of Hong Kong, Chris Patten.

When a fourteen-year-old supporter was shot dead when fighting broke out after Flamengo beat Vasco 4–0 at Rio's Maracana Stadium in October 2000, a police spokesman commented sympathetically: 'That's what happens after the

excitement of the game. In the confusion and euphoria, people get too worked up.'

'I'd give my life to play the Final again tomorrow.' Er . . . yes . . . Valencia's Hector Cuper, obviously somewhat confused after they had lost the 2000 Champions League Final to Real Madrid.

Asked in a match-day programme what profession he would have followed had he not become a footballer, Kidderminster's John Durnin answered in November 2000: 'A mass murderer.'

'I like looking at dead bodies,' declared striker Chris Sutton in the *Chelsea* magazine in September 1999, explaining why his choice of an alternative profession had been 'funeral director'.

'It's been easy for Manchester United, but let me tell you something about next year, we'll be right up there with them. I'll kill myself if we're not challenging them' . . . Olivier Dacourt of Leeds United, March 2001.

'I think a lot of people would agree that some criminals should be beheaded for the things they've done – that's especially true for murderers' . . . Spurs' Matthew Etherington.

'The France team remains very important for me. I want to play at the 2002 World Cup, even if I have to kill somebody for it' . . . AC Milan winger Ibrahim Ba, quoted in February 2001.

'Nothing would stop me going to the Cup Final unless I was dead. And if I was dead, I'd want my ashes taken there.' Many might well agree with Minister for Sport Tony Banks' comments before the 1997 Cup Final, won by his beloved Chelsea.

'If my parents were alive today, they would die of shame' – Romanian star Gheorghe Hagi in April 2001 after discovering that an interview with him had appeared in pornographic magazine *Hustler*.

'Tragic events like this happen everywhere' . . . almost incomprehensibly insensitive statement from Markus Siegler, a FIFA spokesman who was being asked whether the World Cup would still be Africa bound in 2010, after 120 people were killed in a stadium panic in Ghana in May 2001. Commented respected *Daily Mail* writer Ian Wooldridge: 'It was a callous and devastatingly stupid remark.'

'The first person who dropped a piece of litter or was guilty of graffiti should be shot dead' – former Watford boss Graham Taylor talking to Radio 5 Live's Simon Mayo in May 2001.

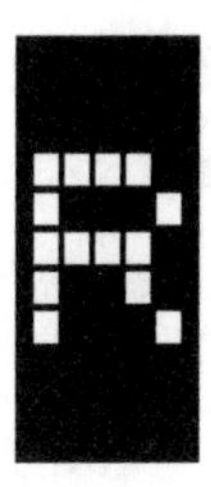

REALLY MADRIP?

Following Real Madrid's Champions League elimination by Dynamo Kiev in 1999, the front page of Catalan daily *Sport*, whose readers are overwhelmingly fans of Real's bitter rivals Barcelona, consisted of one word . . . 'MADR.I.P.'

REF ROUGH STUFF

Czech ref Roman Berbr fled the country in 1995, after receiving an anonymous call warning him that his daughter would be kidnapped and he would suffer a fatal car accident, unless he dropped corruption charges against a member of the Czech FA's Executive Committee.

FIFA were slightly embarrassed when they discovered the referee they had appointed to handle a World Cup qualifier in April 2000 between South Africa and Lesotho had died six months earlier. Zambian officials later confirmed that Boxen Chinagu had been killed in a road accident and was thus unavailable to officiate.

Referee Mick Johnston was buried in his black kit, together with his whistle and a red card, after dying suddenly aged 40 at Teesside in December 1996.

REINCARNATED AS AN OUT-OF-WORK COACH

Surely a contender for the most bizarre dismissal of a national coach, Glenn Hoddle, then in charge of the England side trying to qualify for Euro 2000, was sacked after suggesting in an interview with *The Times* newspaper that disabled people were paying for sins committed in a former life.

As time elapses it seems ever more odd that Hoddle's admittedly awkwardly-expressed opinions should have prompted his dismissal. He said: 'You and I have been physically given two hands and two legs and half-decent brains. Some people have not been born like that for a reason. The karma is working from another lifetime. I have nothing to hide about that. It is not only people with disabilities, what you sow you have to reap.'

A furore quickly built up, although he had previously uttered similar views without any adverse consequences and in essence his beliefs are probably shared by millions around the world. Hoddle himself was soon reincarnated as a coach, doing well at Southampton before moving to Spurs in the spring of 2001.

REPORT

Deaths stemming from football-related violence in Argentina stand at 164 since the start of professional football there in 1931, said a report in *World Soccer* magazine's February 2001 edition.

RIFLE

After Turkish side Galatasaray defeated Paris St Germain 4–2 in the European Cup Winners' Cup in October 1996, an eleven-year-old fan celebrated by firing a barrage from the family hunting rifle – killing his thirteen-year-old sister.

RIOT

A July 1996 League match in Tripoli, Libya, exploded into violence which resulted in the deaths of up to 50 people. The referee allowed a goal for Al-Ahli, scored against bitter rivals Al-Ittihad, to stand. Al-Ittihad supporters invaded the pitch to demonstrate against both the goal and Al-Ahli's owner, the son of Libyan leader Colonel Gaddafi. The referee was reportedly stabbed to death and the two teams were subsequently disbanded.

ROSE

Arsenal fan Tina Evans lays a red rose under her deceased mother's seat at Highbury on the anniversary of her death, birth and at Christmas.

RUMOURS OF MY DEMISE . . .

HFS Loans League side Congleton organised a minute's silence for 27 February, 1993, to mark the passing of long-standing supporter, 85-year-old Fred Cope, who surprised everyone by arriving to watch the match with Rossendale and was himself surprised on reading of his demise in the programme. Confusion between Fred and another recently departed fan was to blame.

Under the heading 'Dead Footballer Not Dead After All', Peter van Dyck, who runs an Internet site devoted to the delights of Colombia, issued an apology on 4 June, 2000: 'A small mistake in our Medellin guide: the footballer killed was "Andres" Escobar, not Geraldo.'

Stunned relatives of James Corr, 78, were told he had died after being taken into South Tyneside Hospital in June 2000. His grandson's wife, April, took a walk around the hospital corridors to clear her thoughts – and found him watching England playing Germany in the TV room.

Belgium's Euro 2000 star midfielder Yves Van Der Haeghe revealed that he once lapsed into a coma, and was reported to have died. Playing at the time for Rosselare, he suffered a brain tumour and club officials actually announced before a League game that he had passed away.

'You should be dead' . . . Professor David Lloyd Griffiths, orthopaedic surgeon, told Manchester City's German keeper Bert Trautmann, who discovered four days after the 1956 Cup Final that he had broken his neck during the game. Trautmann was used to such narrow escapes – as a member of the Luftwaffe's parachute regiment during the war he was captured by the Russians; escaped; re-captured by the French resistance; escaped; survived when a hand grenade blew up in his face; escaped again from American GIs who took pity on him and only pretended to execute him.

A man given the kiss of life by Janet Painter, wife of Stafford Rangers' boss Ian, was clinically dead – yet 48 hours later he

walked out of hospital. The twenty-year-old was amongst fans who swarmed on to the pitch after Stafford beat Solihull in May 2000, to clinch the Doc Martens League Western Division title.

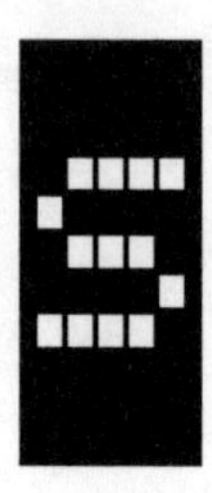

SACRIFICE

'When I made my debut for Besiktas in Turkey, they sacrificed a lamb on the pitch. Its blood was daubed on my forehead and boots to bring me good luck. They never did that at QPR' . . . Les Ferdinand.

SAINTS ALIVE?

The Times reported on 16 March 1998 that the Vatican was set to declare a Bulgarian bishop, killed in 1952 for opposing Stalin's anti-religious laws, the patron saint of football. The Vatican, already boasting its own football league, commented via its five-a-side team manager, Roberto di Stefano: 'We already have a bit of help from above here, but a few extra prayers could not do any harm.'

The issue came up again in September 2000, when legendary Spanish footballer Manolo Garnica, who scored the goal which won the 1911 Cup victory for his club Atletico Madrid over Espanol (but was executed by firing squad during the Civil War) was proposed by the church for beatification. This was a step towards sainthood, and

immortality as the patron saint of football, causing Atletico president Jesus Gil to comment: 'We have established divine contacts who can hear our prayers – knowing we have such an important ally in Heaven will show the Devil himself that Atletico de Madrid cannot stay in his kingdom for ever.'

SCARF

Actress Grace Kelly was a Barcelona fan, given a silk scarf by the club after they played a game in Monaco, to commemorate her wedding. When she died, her daughter Princess Caroline wore the same scarf.

SICK AS A DEAD UN?

Ever wondered where the football cliché 'sick as a parrot' came from? In 1909 Spurs were returning home from a tour of Argentina and Uruguay. On the cruise ship home a fancy dress contest was held – jointly won by two Spurs players who dressed up as Robinson Crusoe and Man Friday – complete with live parrot, supplied by ship officials and gifted to the players concerned.

Ten years later Arsenal controversially replaced Spurs in the First Division – on the very same day the parrot perished, expired, became deceased, went to meet its maker, pegged it, shuffled off this mortal coil, popped off, died. Consequently, Spurs were sick as . . .

SILENCE

The impact of the one-minute silence to honour recently deceased England manager Alf Ramsey, at an England Under-21 game played at Huddersfield's McAlpine Stadium in June 1999, was slightly diminished when the 13,000 crowd

saw the scoreboard flash up a message honouring Manchester United boss Sir Matt Busby by mistake.

SILENT – BUT NOT DEADLY

Mick Harfield had suffered the grievous loss of his young wife, Rosina, the day before turning out for Braishfield, his local Saturday team, reported the *Romsey Advertiser* on 21 March, 1975. He even took part in a two-minute silence before the match then turned in a storming performance in the game. The next week's paper carried an apology to Mrs Harfield: 'She is fit and well and we would like to apologise to her for any upset the report could have caused.'

SILENT PROTEST

The telephone lines were humming in April 2001 when national radio station TalkSport's Mike Parry invited listeners to comment on his opinion that one-minute silences were becoming devalued, after a Spurs fan rang it to say that he had attended three different matches, at all of which a minute's silence had been held in honour of recently deceased Nationwide League ref Mike North, 40, who collapsed and died whilst officiating a game at Southend against Mansfield.

Parry found himself pilloried by many callers. His sidekick presenter, Alan Brazil, the former Ipswich, Man U and Scotland star, disassociated himself from his colleague's controversial point of view that holding silences at Premiership grounds was going too far to honour the ref, and that local recognition should suffice other than for genuinely national disasters or tragedies.

SKULL

A children's football game in the Belgian city of Ghent was cut short by police, who confiscated their 'football' in August 1997. It turned out to be a human skull which had been unearthed from a nearby disused cemetery during the course of roadworks.

SOCCER DEATHS – WHO CARES?

Steve Rushin, a writer for the prrestigious Sports Illustrated magazine in America, wrote a hard hitting piece about football stadium disaster deaths and their lack of impact on Americans, in the May 21, 2001 edition. Soccer stadium catastrophes have become "a Stalinesque statistical litany with little resonance" he claimed, "It is nearly impossible to interest a great many Americans in events overseas" he said.

"Surely no sport – other than soccer – would tolerate so many fatalities among its spectators" he declared, adding, "These are unnatural disasters, not acts of God: they are eminently preventable."

Rushin closed his piece by quoting John Donne – "'Therefore, never send to know for whom the bell tolls.' Sports fans, it tolls for thee."

SPONSORS

Sandhurst Under 13s team were dead pleased with their new shirt sponsors for season 1998–99 – a Camberley firm of funeral directors.

Aberdeen pub team Byron Munich, whose club badge is a skull and crossbones, clinched an appropriate sponsorship deal in September 2000 when they teamed up with funeral

directors William Gilchrist, who supplied the team, from the Lord Byron pub, with black shirts.

Still turning out aged 41 for Cheltenham Town in 1998, former Chelsea winger Clive Walker was sponsored by Beechwood Funeral Directors.

STADIUM

The Aldo Oliveri Stadium was designed to be the perfect memorial for one of Italy's greatest football heroes. The stadium in Verona was to be dedicated to the memory of the keeper who sealed Italy's 1938 World Cup triumph. The weekend before the opening ceremony at the stadium, in 1996, a small problem was revealed – Aldo wasn't dead. At 86, he was still alive and in good health.

STIFFS

Newcastle punter Steve Irons caused a storm in January 1994 when he cashed in on Sir Matt Busby's death by winning £1320 in a Celebrity Stiffs sweepstake. Steve, and other gamblers, paid 50p per week into a kitty, with the cash going to the first one to nominate successfully a well known figure who subsequently died. Bobby Charlton was not best pleased to learn of the win: 'It is sick – they are debasing the memory of a great man,' he commented.

SUB HUMAN?

The Sun reported on 22 January, 2001, that 'Manchester United have appealed to their fans to stop a sick song about the Russian submarine disaster. The lyrics compare the

possible fate of neighbours Manchester City to the loss of the *Kursk*, which sank in August last year. All 118 on board died.' An article in the United programme also deplored the use of the song: 'This is a wholly inappropriate link, and one which most United supporters find most distasteful and short on humour.' In late 2001, a Celtic fan was reportedly banned by the club after taunting an opposing American player by imitating a crashing aeroplane, shortly after the World Trade Centre tragedy.

SUICIDE

Late nineteenth-century Newcastle keeper Charles Watts retired in 1906, becoming a professional racing tipster. Perhaps the winners dried up, as in 1924 he committed suicide by cutting his throat.

Hughie Ferguson, who scored the winning goal in the FA Cup Final for Cardiff against Arsenal, and who established a British record total of 362 League goals, became a sad figure who committed suicide aged 34 on 9 January, 1930. He had fallen into a state of depression about his comparative failure at Dundee, which had led to barracking from supporters. On that day, he attended a training session at Dens Park, after which he gassed himself.

Barcelona FC's founder Hans Gamper-Haessing committed suicide on 13 October, 1930.

Having earlier begun pre-season training with the rest of the squad, Crystal Palace keeper Billy Callender killed himself in Selhurst Park dressing room in July 1932, following the recent death of his fiancée.

West Ham's first manager, Syd King, was sacked in November 1932 and, a month later, committed suicide 'by consuming an alcoholic beverage laced with a corrosive liquid.'

The decapitated body of Scottish international striker Hughie Gallagher, (born 1903) who had played for Queen of the South, Airdrie, Newcastle, Chelsea, Derby, Notts Co, Grimsby and Gateshead, was found at Dead Man's Crossing, Low Fell, after he threw himself under the York-Edinburgh express on the morning of 11 June, 1957. Gallagher was facing legal proceedings at Gateshead for the alleged maltreatment of his son, a charge later described as 'nonsense' by sports historian Paul Joannou, who researched his life.

Erich Schaedler, son of a German prisoner of war, played for Hibs in the early 1970s, winning a cap for Scotland against West Germany in 1974, but after retiring from the game, committed suicide.

When Rangers player Bobby McKean committed suicide by inhaling fumes from the exhaust of his car, some Celtic fans responded with a song based on the old Middle of the Road group's 'Chirpy, Chirpy, Cheep, Cheep', – 'Where's your Bobby gone, He's left his engine on.' An equally respectful element of Rangers' fans took their revenge when Celtic's Johnny Doyle was electrocuted in October 1981, apparently whilst working on a loft extension. They sang, to the tune of Lesley Gore's 'It's My Party' – 'It's my attic and I'll fry if I want to.'

Former England international Dave Clements, of QPR and Bolton, committed suicide on 31 March, 1982.

After being dropped for the first time in six seasons, Abdon Porte, centre half for Uruguayan club, Nacional, committed suicide in the centre of their Parque Central pitch.

Twenty-seven-year-old Mehmet Dalman hanged himself from a tree following his Turkish side Trabzonspor's top of the table defeat against Fenerbahce in May 1996. In his pocket was a request to be buried in a coffin draped with club colours.

Former England Under 21 star Justin Fashanu, brother of John, who played for Forest, Southampton, Notts County and Brighton, committed suicide in May 1998 at the age of 37.

A Lazio fan killed himself in June 1999 after his favourite side sold their star player, Christian Vieri, for a reported £30 million. The fan, 25-year-old Elio Di Cristofalo, threw himself under a train in Rome and was decapitated. A suicide note, discovered later, read, 'I don't even know why I am still alive, Lazio have sold Vieri. All that money for a footballer, but money is not everything in life.'

Twenty-six-year-old Carlos Montoya, centre back for top Colombian club, America, hanged himself in December 1999.

When Romanian Second Division player Mihai Baica's dream move from Foresta Sucara to Italian side Genoa fell through in late summer 2000, because club officials accepted a rival bid from a Romanian side, his wife took an overdose and attempted suicide – only to be saved when her mother in law returned home early from a shopping trip.

Mirco Saric, of Argentinian club San Lorenzo, committed suicide in April 2000. In 1981, defender Hugo Pena, from the same club, was bathing his foot in a basin when he switched on a TV and was electrocuted. Four years later the club's midfielder Jorge Coufanes was shot dead by muggers. In 1991 their striker Ruben Bernuncio crashed his car into a bus and died.

A Nigerian man killed himself when the national side could only draw 0–0 in a World Cup qualifier with Ghana in March 2001. The middle-aged fan had threatened to commit suicide in his home town of Umuahia if Nigeria did not win the game in Accra. Said witness Joyce Onwuka, 'When he said it we thought he was joking. But immediately after the match he took out a small bottle and drank the contents. It was when he started foaming at the mouth a few minutes later and subsequently died that we realised it was not a joke.'

TEAM TALK

'Win or die' said Mussolini's telegram to the Italian team before the Final of the 1938 World Cup against Hungary. They won, and defeated captain Antal Szabo remarked: 'I have never felt so proud in my life. We may have lost the match, but we have saved eleven lives.'

THE MAN WHO KILLED THE MAN WHO KILLED THE MAN

Team names seem to be elusive, but a number of reports exist relating that during a South American game in April 1962 a spectator stabbed the referee to death, whereupon another spectator shot the first spectator, after which panic set in, the crowd headed for the exits – and another spectator was crushed to death.

TOBY . . . OR NOT TOBY

Scottish club Morton landed a meaty sponsorship deal with

a local butcher who donated a lamb every time they scored during the 1910–11 season. Centre forward Tommy Gracies kept one, which subsequently became the club mascot – only to 'meat' a sorry end when it was found drowned in the club bath. Theories as to how and why are as many and inventive as you could imagine.

TOMBSTONE

In January 1997, TV commentator Kenneth Wolstenholme, then 76, revealed that a friend had arranged to have a tombstone engraved for him, featuring the famous phrase he had uttered whilst commentating on the 1966 World Cup Final: 'They think it's all over . . . It is now.'

TRAIN DEAD

After winning at Atletico Madrid to clinch their promotion in 1934, nine Sevilla supporters died and over a hundred more were injured when the train taking them home crashed.

Six fans being chased by police for unruly behaviour were killed by a train as they crossed a railway line in Jakarta in April 1999.

Burnley's first full-time manager, Spence Whittaker, died in April 1910 when he fell from a train carriage at Crewe whilst en route to London to register the details of a new signing for the club.

TRAITOR

Skipper of the French team in the 1930 World Cup Final, right half Alex Villaplane was ultimately shot by the French resistance for collaborating with the Nazis.

TRANSFER OF DEATH

Barcelona President Josep Sunyol is said by author Julian Garcia-Candau to have met his death in August 1936 during Civil War hostilities, when he went to offer a former Oviedo player who was involved in the conflict a contract to play for Barca when it was all over. Sunyol fell foul of Falangist troops and was gunned down. His body was exhumed in the 1990s for the club to mark the 60th anniversary of his death.

TV

Chinese doctors warned the elderly to limit the amount of football they watched on TV during the 1998 World Cup after the death was reported in the *Guangzhou Daily Reporter* of an elderly man called Ni, who had taken to sleeping during the day and staying up all night to watch matches live from France. He succumbed to a heart attack as Brazil beat Morocco.

VC

When Second Lieutenant Donald Bell spotted a German machine-gun post during the 1916 Battle of the Somme, he did not stop to think, but ran at it, throwing grenades with his left hand and firing his revolver with his right. The action of the former Bradford Park Avenue player saved the lives of fellow soldiers in the Green Howards, and he became the only professional footballer to be awarded the Victoria Cross. He died, though, five days later, leading a charge over the top. In 2000 Bell was honoured at a full military ceremony in France to commemorate his heroism. The Professional Footballers' Association paid for a permanent memorial to him.

Former Third Lanark player John Ferguson of the fourth Cameronians, 'took out three enemy machine-guns and cleared a 200 yard trench in October 1916' before being killed, reported *The Daily Express*. His captain, W Wallace, recommended him for a posthumous VC, which never materialised.

John Readitt, 17, a cobbler, worked with his father supplying football boots to Manchester United, from their shop in Clayton, Manchester, before he enlisted to fight in the First World War for the South Lancashire Regiment. On 25 February, 1917, in Mesopotamia, he defied heavy enemy fire from Turkish machine-gunners, leading advances on the enemy and was awarded a VC in November of 1919, the year in which he was discharged. He returned to work on the ten-year United boot contract, which still had six years to run – and died in Clayton in June 1964.

VODKA

Scarborough FC were once sponsored by Black Death Vodka.

WAR FOOTING

They may not have been the actual cause, but a hotly contested series of three World Cup qualifiers in 1969 were followed by all-out war between neighbouring South American countries El Salvador and Honduras.

The first game in June 1969 in Honduras was won 1–0 by the home country in volatile circumstances, after which a Salvadorian woman committed suicide, resulting in her funeral being shown live on TV and attended by the football team. The next game, a week later was won 3–0 by El Salvador in a hostile atmosphere, and within a week diplomatic links were severed. The play-off took place in Mexico City and was won 3–0 by El Salvador.

Two weeks later, on 14 July, 1969 El Salvador invaded Honduras, sparking a conflict in which over 2,000 died. Gerard Reid, whose book *Football War* covered this event, commented 'these games would provide the flint to the spark for the war.'

WAR VICTIMS

An Internet site called Scottish Footballers in the Great War and reached at *www.geocities.com/Athens/Pantheon/*3828, tells some tragic tales of footballers who perished during the First World War.

In November 1914 the entire sixteen-man first team squad of Hearts of Midlothian FC enlisted en masse. Seven Hearts players subsequently died. Private James Hodge Speedie died aged 21 on 25 September, 1915, during a 'Big push at Loos'. His body was never found. Corporal Tom Gracie is the only Hearts player to die during the First World War who has a known grave, having been transferred to hospital in Glasgow after being taken ill and dying on 23 October, 1915, aged 26.

At the Battle of the Somme, four Hearts players died – Private Henry Wattie; Sergeant Duncan Currie; Private Ernest Ellis and the last Hearts man to die on the Somme, Lance Corporal James Boyd. Gunner Robert Mercer, gassed in the war, died in a friendly against Selkirk on 23 April, 1926.

Believed to be the last British soldier killed in the First World War, George Brooks, a Derby County player, died on Armistice Day in 1918.

Fulham stalwart Jimmy Tompkins rose to the rank of major but was killed on D-Day in Normandy. The club's winger Dennis Higgins was killed in North Africa in 1942, while young players George Fairburn and Ernie Tuckett also perished in the conflict.

Manchester City inside forward Alex 'Sandy' Turnbull, who later joined Manchester United, winning the FA Cup with both, joined the Manchester Regiment and was killed at

Arras on 3 May, 1917. United's Ben Carpenter was a Second World War casualty.

Manchester City player Alfred Keeling was declared missing, presumed killed, as an RAF fighter pilot in December 1942.

Reported missing believed killed in action in April 1945, Wolves player Alec McIntosh had been captured and survived as a prisoner of war. Blackpool's Corporal Alec Munro was reported missing in the Middle East in July 1942, only to be discovered as a POW in Italy.

Arsenal's Fusilier Hugh Glass was drowned at sea in 1943; their Spitfire pilot RAF Flight Sergeant Leslie Lack was reported missing also in 1943; another Gunner, Flying Officer Sidney Pugh, was killed on active service in 1944 while Bill Dean, who had played in goal for Arsenal, died in action with the Navy in March 1942.

A number of former Celtic players died during the First World War – Private John McLaughlin was killed in action at the Somme on 13 November, 1916; Private Robert Craig died of wounds in Boulogne on 19 April, 1918; Private Peter Johnstone, who played in the 1914 Cup Final for Celtic, was killed in action at Arras on 16 May, 1916 aged 26; Gunner Donald McLeod of the Royal Field Artillery who played for Celtic between 1902–8, was killed in action on 6 October, 1917, and is buried in Dozingham Military Cemetery.

Seven Kilmarnock players were killed in the Great War – Corporal David Slimmon, killed in action on 23 July, 1917, aged 21; Lance Sergeant Alexander McCurdie, killed in

action 24 April, 1917, aged 22; Daniel McKellar, Charles Vickers, Alexander Barrie, John Rollo, Andre D. Armour.

Several Raith Rovers players were killed on active service – Sergeant George McLay, killed at the battle of Passchendaele, 22 October, 1917, awarded a posthumous Military Medal for 'conspicuous bravery', aged 26. Private James Todd was killed in action on 12 March, 1916, aged 20.

Corporal John Bellringer, an Ayr United player, was killed in action on 12 July, 1915, aged 23. Private Robert Capperauld of the same club died of wounds on 14 July, 1915; goalkeeper, Private Samuel Herbertson died on 12 July, 1915; Private Thomas Clifford of Ayr, Celtic, Luton Town, Nottingham Forest and Motherwell, died on 19 January, 1917, aged 42.

Dumbarton player Private Harry Gildea was killed in action on 9 April, 1917.

Tommy Goodwill, a Newcastle midfielder with 60 appearances to his credit, was killed whilst serving with the Northumberland Fusiliers during the First World War.

Yugoslav patriots invaded a football ground where a match was taking place between Italians and Croats in September 1942, killing the Italian referee and six Italian players.

Albania's Stadium Qemal Stafa in the capital, Tirana, is named after the writer of that name, founder of the Albanian Communist Party, who was killed in May 1942, aged 22, by the occupying Italian forces.

Lord Ninian Crichton-Stuart, after whom Cardiff's ground was named, was killed in action in Belgium in October 1915. Cardiff players Tom Witts and James McKenzie perished during the First World War.

Sunderland's flamboyant keeper Leigh Richmond Roose and full back Albert Milton both died during the First World War. Roose won 24 caps for Wales and also played for Stoke and Everton, before going off to war with the 9th Battalion Royal Fusiliers. He saw action and was killed on 7 October, 1916 on the Somme, being awarded a posthumous Military Medal.

West Ham players Arthur Stallard, Bill Kennedy, Frank Costello and Frank Cannon were all First World War victims.

Luton Town players who died during the First World War were full back Jack Jarvis, striker Arthur H. Whiteman, Ernest J. Dodds, Frank Gilder and George Porter.

Lieutenant Walter 'Darkie' Tull was killed in action at the second Battle of the Somme on March 25, 1918 and subsequently received a posthumous Military Cross. He was the British Army's first black officer – and in 1909 became one of the country's first black professional footballers, when he turned out for Rangers, Spurs and Northampton.

Chelsea's Alexander Skinner Jackson, nicknamed the Gay Cavalier, was killed in a road accident in Cairo in 1946 whilst serving in the army as a major.

WATERFALL

Former Real Madrid and Oviedo player Petr Dubovsky was reported to have died in June 2000 in an accident whilst on holiday in Thailand. Dubovsky, his girlfriend, sister and brother-in-law were sightseeing at a 20-metre-high waterfall on the island of Koh Samui, when the player slipped and fell whilst taking photographs, hitting his head on rocks below and dying shortly afterwards, said one report. Another claimed that the 28-year-old, with 33 caps to his name for Slovakia, had jumped from a 30-foot-high rock. Yet another version of the tragedy was bizarrely headlined 'Slovakia Star Killed by Leonardo DiCaprio' – the actor had apparently jumped at a similar waterfall in his movie *The Beach*.

WATER WAY TO GO

Benfica player Luciano was reported to have died when he was electrocuted in the club jacuzzi on 5 December, 1966.

WEB DEAD

Internet site *www.findagrave.com* was set up to co-ordinate details of the final resting places of major sports stars. Being compiled from mainly non-British sources, the footballers listed are not always immediately familiar to a British audience. When I visited the site I discovered that former Inter and Sampdoria player Lennart 'Nacka' Skoglund (1929–75) is buried in Skogskyrkogarden, Stockholm; and that footballer and 'hero of Socialist Labour' Nikolai Petrovich Starostin is interred at Vakangovskoye Cemetery in Moscow. There appeared to be few other soccer players immortalised.

WHAT A BOER!

After just nine games for Man U forerunner Newton Heath, Gilbert Godsmark was called up for the Boer War. The club kept up his registration, only to be informed in February that he had been killed in action. He had signed for Newton Heath from Ashford FC who had received half of the agreed fee of £40 – and then had to sue for the rest after Newton Heath claimed they weren't liable for it as Godsmark had only been on trial with them.

WHISTLED OUT

Sam Cowan, FA Cup winning centre half with Manchester City, died aged 63 whilst refereeing a charity match. Liverpool's Joe Dines, winner of an Olympic Gold Medal in 1912, was killed in action on the Western Front, while their winger Wilfred Bartrop was a fatality late in the same conflict.

WHODUNNIT?

The 1938 Arsenal team played themselves in a murder whodunnit film *The Arsenal Stadium Mystery* in which the striker from an amateur team taking on the Gunners drops dead on the pitch.

WILL POWER

Fulham fan Yorky Whiting, 59, vowed to leave everything he owned to Fulham in his 1966 will, reported Dean Hayes in his 2000 book *The Craven Cottage Encyclopaedia* adding that amongst the 'everything' the Devon dustman possessed were a house painted in Fulham colours, a garage fronted by a set

of goalposts, a carriage lamp bearing the likeness of player Johnny Haynes, and interior décor consisting of hundreds of Fulham programmes.

An anonymous mathematics professor's death in 1984 added up to good news for Brazilian club Bangu, who were pleasantly surprised to be left £250,000 in his will. It transpired that the nutty prof had once attended a Carnival in the town and fallen in love with a young girl from there. Having no direct relatives to hand his cash over to, he had opted sentimentally for the club from the love of his life's town to benefit.

It was revealed in February 1998 that 60-year-old decorator Ken Selwyn, who died of a stroke, had left his £73,000 house to cash-strapped Gloucester City FC, of the Doc Martens League, his life-long favourite team.

WINDOW TRIBUTE

The Duncan Edwards window in the parish church of St Francis in Dudley, Worcestershire, his hometown, is a stained glass tribute to the brilliant young Manchester United and England defender who perished as a result of the Munich air crash. A book, *Tackle Soccer This Way*, which Edwards had finished writing just before the trip, was posthumously published in June 1958 with proceeds donated by the publisher to the Lord Mayor of Manchester's Fund for dependants of those who lost their lives in the crash.

WINNING TICKET

When popular Scottish religious figure Cardinal Thomas Winning (1925–2001) was buried in June of the latter year, the Daily Record reported: 'Cardinal Winning was laid to rest in the way he would have wanted – with his ticket from Celtic's cup final win up his sleeve. His nephew put it there before the funeral.'

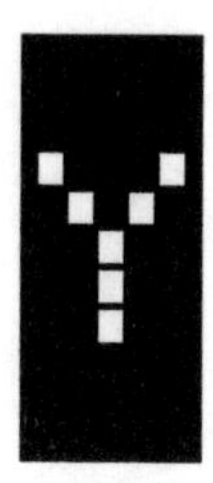

YACHT A WAY TO GO

Rangers manager for over twenty years, William Wilton died, when he fell overboard from a friend's yacht in heavy seas, on May 2, 1920.

YOU'RE GOING NOWHERE

Reading trainer Glenn Hunter brought winger Andy Rogers back to life, after he stopped breathing for 90 seconds when he suffered a fit following a collision during a game against Swansea, on February 22, 1986.

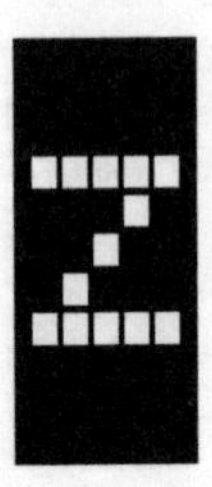

ZUNIGA'S FATAL SWITCH

In 1977 Libardo Zuniga, winger for Santa Rosa de Cabal, took over in goal after their keeper for the Colombian Second Division game was injured. The stand-in keeper performed brilliantly, outraging the opposing striker, who kicked him in the groin – a blow from which he subsequently died.

1 January 1970 . . . Former Spurs, Norwich and Chester player Andrew Thompson died aged 70.

1 January 1972 . . . Former Third Lanark, Spurs and Sheffield United forward John Blair died aged 66.

1 January 1998 . . . Former Preston striker Dennis Hatsell died aged 67.

2 January 1971 . . . Sixty-six died and 145 were injured as a result of a stairway crush during the Rangers-Celtic League match at Ibrox.

3 January 1958 . . . Fred Thompson, FA Cup winning keeper with Bury in 1900, died aged 86.

3 January 1971 . . . Former Wolves, Norwich and Palace full back Albert Thorpe died aged 60.

3 January 1968 . . . Former Spurs player and York manager Jimmy McCormick died following a road accident in Spain, aged 55.

3 January 1969 . . . Former Norwich, Blackburn, Southend and Clapton Orient full back Philip Hope died aged 71.

3 January 1977 . . . Former Falkirk, Motherwell and Portsmouth left back James Mackrell died aged 71.

4 January 1998 . . . Former Mansfield, Huddersfield, Barnsley, Lincoln and Doncaster centre half John Sanders died aged 47.

5 January 1998 . . . Wicket keeper for Yorkshire and England, David Bairstow, who played 17 League games for Bradford City, died aged 46.

6 January 1934 . . . Gunners boss Herbert Chapman, who persuaded London Transport to rename Gillespie Road tube station Arsenal, died aged 54.

6 January 1957 . . . Former Barnsley and Norwich winger George Dobson died aged 55.

6 January 1966 . . . Former Forest, Norwich, Blackpool and Halifax left back Ernest Gadsden died aged 70.

6 January 1982 . . . Former Norwich, Luton Town, Spurs and Southend inside right Samuel Bell died aged 73.

6 January 1997 . . . Former Newcastle player John Eric Garbutt died aged 76.

6 January 1997 . . . Spurs, Chelsea and Brentford full back Sid Tickridge died aged 73.

6 January 1998 . . . Former Burnley full back John 'Jolly Jack' Marshall, England trainer in the late fifties died aged 80.

7 January 1940 . . . Former Coventry, Brentford, Newcastle, Norwich, Brighton, Manchester City and Crewe centre forward Jack Doran – who was awarded the DCM and Military Medal in the First World War – died aged 44.

7 January 1967 . . . Left back for Norwich in eight Football League games William Dempsey died aged 70.

8 January 1998 . . . Former Tranmere forward Gilbert Alldis died aged 77.

8 January 2000 . . . Former Bristol City wing half William Tovey died aged 68.

9 January 1959 . . . Irish international and former Everton, Spurs, Chelsea, Clyde and Leyton Orient player John Kirwan died aged 80.

9 January 1994 . . . Scots-born James Brown, who returned from the US to England after the Wall Street Crash and played for Manchester United, Brentford and Spurs, died aged 85.

9 January 1995 . . . Rochdale, Villa, Swindon and Gillingham half back William Armstrong died aged 82.

10 January 1995 . . . Spurs half back Albert Page died aged 78.

10 January 1997 . . . Scottish international centre half – 53 caps – George Young, who won six League titles, four Scottish Cups and two League Cups with Rangers, died aged 74. Never cautioned or dismissed.

10 January 1999 . . . Former Walsall and Swindon player Ken Goldstraw died aged 81.

11 January 1962 . . . Former Norwich and Peterborough inside forward Cyril Dunning died aged 63.

11 January 1983 . . . Former Exeter, Norwich, Swindon and Luton forward Fred Dent died aged 86.

11 January 1996 . . . Newcastle full back for thirteen years, George Coldwell died aged 73.

11 January 1997 . . . Long-serving Queen of the South keeper Roy Henderson died aged 73.

12 January 1980 . . . Middlesbrough drew 1–1 at home with Manchester United. Immediately after the game at Ayresome Park a gate collapsed, killing two spectators.

12 January 1983 . . . Cecil Poynton, with Spurs for over 50 years as player, trainer and physio, died aged 81.

12 January 1994 . . . Former Stoke, Southport, Crewe player and Oxford manager, Arthur Turner died aged 85.

12 January 1997 . . . Former Birmingham, Coventry and Walsall wing half turned inside forward, Don Dorman died aged 74.

12 January 1998 . . . Former top scorer in Scotland in 1969–70, for Cowdenbeath, John Dickson later joined St Mirren and Ayr. He died aged 49.

12 January 1998 . . . Former Stoke, Spurs, Orient and Bolton player Ian Moores died aged 43

13 January 1984 . . . Former Hibs, Liverpool and Scotland keeper Tommy Younger died aged 54.

13 January 1991 . . . Forty fans trampled to death as fighting broke out at match in Orkney, 80 miles from Johannesburg, after ref allowed disputed first goal of game for Kaiser Chiefs against Orlando Pirates, sparking disturbances.

14 January 1914 . . . Bristol City fans tried to unsettle visiting FA Cup opponents QPR by printing 'In Memoriam' cards predicting their imminent demise. QPR won 2–0.

14 January 1958 . . . Newcastle striker Bill Appleyard, who in the early 1900s averaged a goal every other game, died.

14 January 1991 . . . John Houghton nearly became a centenarian, but the former Rangers, Norwich and Fulham full back died in California four months short of his 100th birthday.

15 January 1917 . . . Former Chelsea player Benjamin Warren died after having been certified insane and spending time in a lunatic asylum.

15 January 1961 . . . Former Norwich winger John Cutmore died in Australia, aged 75.

15 January 1975 . . . Former Norwich centre forward Thomas Hunt died aged 66.

16 January 1996 . . . Former Burnley player and manager, Harry Potts died aged 75.

17 January 1951 . . . Former Forest, Norwich, West Ham and Brighton – for whom he played the final match of his career on his 28th birthday – centre half Oliver Brown died aged 42.

17 January 1969 . . . Former Chelsea and QPR player Samuel Irving died aged 85.

18 January 1981 . . . Former Newcastle manager Duggie Livingstone died aged 82.

18 January 1982 . . . Newcastle full back turned youth team coach, Benny Craig died aged 66.

18 January 1999 . . . Southampton, Exeter, Dundee United defender Percy Ames died aged 77.

19 January 1963 . . . Former Norwich, Luton Town and Millwall winger Ernest Coxhead – who at one stage of his career turned out for Norwich under the name A. Canary in order that his anti-football father should not know he was playing – died aged 76.

19 January 1977 . . . Former Rangers keeper and East Fife manager Jerry Dawson died aged 68.

20 January 1929 . . . Former Spurs defender Ollie Burton died aged 49.

20 January 1979 . . . Newcastle defender Bill McCracken, who spent nineteen years with the club, winning three League titles and the FA Cup died aged 95.

20 January 1984 . . . Ernest Coleman, former prolific scorer for Grimsby, Arsenal, Middlesbrough, Norwich, and manager of Notts County, died aged 76.

20 January 1994 . . . Manchester United legend Sir Matt Busby died aged 84.

21 January 1993 . . . Winger George Edwards, winner of the War Cup in 1944 with Villa, who scored 147 goals in 284 matches for Villa and who was also a talented runner, swimmer, snooker and billiards player, died aged 74.

22 January 1972 . . . Former Birmingham, Southampton, Spurs, Middlesbrough and Watford player Jack Elkes died aged 78.

22 January 1989 . . . Former Sunderland, Norwich and Barrow keeper Robert Robinson died aged 78.

22 January 1998 . . . Former Raith and Third Lanark player Johnny Maule died aged 76.

23 January 1991 . . . Former six-times Leyton Orient boss – it was his party – Les Gore died aged 77.

24 January 1976 . . . Bob Pailor, a forward transferred from WBA to Newcastle, died aged 88.

25 January 1943 . . . Despite being the first Norwich keeper to play 100 League games they transfer-listed Charles

Dennington 'for intemperate habits' – I'll drink to that! He joined Bradford City and died aged 43.

26 January 1943 . . . John Bowman, former Norwich player and their first-ever manager, died aged 63.

26 January 1995 . . . Former Everton and Sunderland full back John Jones died aged 81.

28 January 1933 . . . Former Blackburn and Norwich centre half Sam Wolstenholme died aged 54.

28 January 1995 . . . Former Grimbsy, Scunthorpe centre half and Villa manager Richard Taylor died aged 77.

29 January 1982 . . . Once rewarded with a gold sovereign by Norwich chairman Ernie Morse for admitting to the referee that a goal he'd scored should be ruled out, Percy Varco, a centre forward also with Villa, QPR and Exeter, died aged 77.

29 January 1994 . . . Former Crewe wing half turned Stoke manager, Tony Waddington died aged 69.

30 January 1965 . . . Football fixtures cancelled for funeral of Sir Winston Churchill.

30 January 1983 . . . Former Stockport, Huddersfield, Reading, Spurs and Notts County player Tom Meade died aged 82.

30 January 1986 . . . Gustav Sebes, Hungarian manager when they beat England 6–3 at Wembley, died aged 80.

30 January 2000 . . . On loan to Rushden and Diamonds from Blackpool, forward Martin Aldridge died in a car crash following a match, aged 25.

1 February 1975 . . . When former Norwich half back James Hannah died aged 76, only three players could boast of more appearances for the club – 427. A perfectionist, he once made himself walk home 25 miles after a poor performance.

1 February 1995 . . . Former war-time full back Joe Bacuzzi of Fulham and England died aged 78.

1 February 1998 . . . George Marks of Arsenal, England's first-choice keeper during the Second World War, died aged 82.

2 February 1987 . . . Former Norwich full back Archibald Campbell died aged 89.

2 February 1990 . . . Former Charlton skipper Don Welsh, who won three England caps and managed Brighton, Liverpool and Bournemouth, died aged 78.

2 February 1997 . . . Former Chelsea, Plymouth and Reading winger Wilf Chitty died aged 84.

3 February 1986 . . . Former Everton, Exeter, Norwich and Bristol Rovers inside left Harold 'Happy' Houghton died aged 79.

3 February 1999 . . . Former Hearts, Man City, Notts County, Shrewsbury and Mansfield defender Arthur Mann died aged 51.

4 February 1940 . . . Former Norwich and Blackpool forward Horace 'Moosh' King died aged 56.

4 February 1992 . . . Former Man U, Newcastle, Swansea and Bradford City player Alan Davies committed suicide, aged 30.

4 February 1995 . . . Twenty-three-year-old Brazilian player Augusto Candido suffered a heart attack and died during a game for his Second Division side, Boom.

5 February 1910 . . . Norwich centre half Honrie Reed, 27, left the pitch where he was playing for the Reserves against Brighton and went to the dressing rooms where he died, it later transpired, from an extensively diseased heart.

5 February 1973 . . . Former Millwall, Norwich and Watford inside left Alf Moule died aged 78.

6 February 1958 . . . Twenty-three people, including eight Manchester United players and eight journalists, died as a result of the Munich air crash, which occurred at 3.04pm.

6 February 1976 . . . Former Norwich, Northampton and Torquay inside left Eric Price died aged 71.

6 February 1984 . . . Former Hartlepool and Norwich left half, teetotal Harry Proctor, who later became a pub landlord, died aged 71.

7 February 1934 . . . Keeper for Aston Villa, when they won the double in 1897, Jimmy Whitehouse died aged 60.

8 February 1958 . . . Former Norwich City full back William Cracknell, who boasted the excellently named Norwich Whifflers as a former club, died aged 79.

8 February 1981 . . . Twenty-four male spectators, all aged between 14 and 34, died when a 40,000 crowd rushed from the stadium at Piraeus, Greece, where Olympiakos had beaten AEK Athens 6–0. The stadium capacity was, as a result, cut to 34,300.

9 February 1936 . . . Former Newcastle, Liverpool, Stockport, Swindon and Accrington inside left Arthur Metcalf died aged 46.

9 February 1952 . . . A minute's silence was observed at games around Britain to mark the recent death of King George VI.

9 February 1984 . . . Former New Brighton, Millwall and Norwich centre forward Alex Harley died aged 85.

10 February 1944 . . . Arsenal player Cyril Tooze, serving in the Royal Fusiliers, was killed by a sniper's bullet in Italy.

10 February 1999 . . . Scottish international forward William Houliston died aged 77.

10 February 2000 . . . Former Preston and Hull forward Joseph Horton died aged 77.

14 February 1995 . . . Former West Ham and Chelsea inside forward who became manager of Chelsea and Watford, Len Goulden died aged 82.

14 February 1996 . . . Liverpool's most successful manager Bob Paisley died aged 77.

17 February 1976 . . . Former Chelsea player Thomas Law died.

17 February 1993 . . . Outside left in Pompey's 1949 and 50 championship winning sides, Jack Froggat, who won 13 England caps, died aged 71.

17 February 1998 . . . Former Swansea skipper and centre half, and Derby player-manager Reg Watson died aged 80.

19 February 1934 . . . Former Norwich and Doncaster inside forward William Jex died aged 48.

19 February 1994 . . . Winger Johnny Hancocks, who had three England caps and won the FA Cup and League title with Wolves, died aged 74.

19 February 1998 . . . Former England international and Arsenal full back, George Male died aged 87.

19 February 1999 . . . Scottish international full back, Jock Govan of Hibs and Ayr, died aged 76.

20 February 1976 . . . Former Notts County, Millwall and Norwich half back Arthur Pembleton died aged 81.

20 February 1997 . . . Stan Pearson, the man who scored the winning goal for Manchester United when they beat Blackpool 4–3 in the 1948 FA Cup Final, died aged 78.

21 February 1934 . . . Former Man U, Northampton and Norwich player Tom Smith, whose six brothers were all footballers, died aged 33.

21 February 1958 . . . Two weeks after the Munich air crash Man U star Duncan Edwards, believed by many to have been potentially their greatest player, died from injuries sustained in the disaster.

22 February 1972 . . . Walter Leonard Featherby, who played on the wing for many sides including Norwich, Wolves, Reading, Mansfield, Crewe, Plymouth and Notts County, died aged 66.

22 February 1978 . . . QPR and Leeds Utd manager between 1959–61, John Taylor, of Norwich, Watford, Barnsley and Hull, died aged 64.

22 February 1996 . . . The German manager when they won the 1974 World Cup, Helmut Schon died aged 80.

23 February 1966 . . . Billy Hampson, who brought Bill Shankly to Carlisle when he was boss there and had played for Newcastle and Norwich, died aged 81.

23 February 1995 . . . Former Cardiff and Tranmere winger Seamus McBennett died aged 69.

23 February 2000 . . . Former Arsenal full back Dennis Evans died aged 69.

24 February 1962 . . . Former Norwich half-back William Barclay died aged 68.

24 February 1993 . . . England World Cup winning skipper Bobby Moore, of West Ham, died of cancer aged 51.

24 February 1997 . . . Signed from Morton by Hearts in 1949 for a then-record fee of £100,000, forward Colin Liddell died in his 72nd year.

25 February 1967 . . . Centre half Tony Alden, 23, playing for Highgate United of Worcestershire in an FA Amateur Cup

quarter final against Enfield, was struck by lightning. He died the next day.

25 February 1969 . . . Former Norwich centre forward Theo Randall died aged 84.

25 February 1976 . . . Former West Ham, Norwich and Exeter left half John Gurkin – seldom in a pickle on the park – died aged 80.

26 February 1995 . . . Former Bury, Tranmere, Palace, Watford, Orient and Colchester forward Barry Dyson died aged 52.

27 February 1959 . . . Former Chelsea player Robert McRoberts died.

27 February 1998 . . . Jimmy Hagan, the Sheffield United stalwart, with 400-plus appearances; 15 wartime England caps, one official, who later won the League and Cup double as Benfica boss, died aged 80.

28 February 1956 . . . Former Bradford City and Norwich winger Danny McKinney died aged 57.

28 February 1986 . . . Former Arsenal, Huddersfield, Fulham and England player Pat Beasley died aged 72.

28 February 1990 . . . Former Norwich and Colchester winger

Cliff Birch – who played for Newport and scored for them in the afternoon of the day on which he had wed a Norwich girl in the morning – died aged 61.

1 March 1990 . . . Former Millwall player Dean Horrix died aged 28, in a car crash.

1 March 1999 . . . Outside left Tommy Pearson of Newcastle and Aberdeen, the Scottish international who oddly played for England against Scotland in a wartime international when an England player had a car crash en route, died aged 85.

3 March 1968 . . . Former Norwich winger Robert Baker died aged 84.

3 March 1993 . . . Tony Bland, 22, a victim of the 1989 Hillsborough tragedy, died following a House of Lords judgement which allowed doctors legally to end his life, by removing the feeding tube which had kept him alive for almost four years.

3 March 1997 . . . WBA stalwart – 436 league appearances, seven goals – Len Millard died aged 77.

4 March 1959 . . . Winger-star of Liverpool's title winning teams of 1922 and 1923, Tommy Bromilow died aged 64.

4 March 1981 . . . Former Norwich full back Samuel Bowen died aged 77.

5 March 1946 . . . Thirty-three people died at Burnden Park, when barriers collapsed during a Bolton v Stoke FA Cup quarter final.

5 March 1953 . . . Frank McPherson of Barrow, Man U – where he scored 52 goals – Watford and Reading, died aged 52.

5 March 1997 . . . Former Newcastle centre half Frank Brennan, who won seven Scottish caps, and played in two FA Cup finals, died aged 72.

6 March 1953 . . . Former Leeds, Barnsley and Norwich utility player Joseph Richmond, awarded the French Militaire medal, died aged 55.

6 March 1988 . . . Former Notts County and Norwich full back Ralph Cornwell died aged 86.

6 March 1997 . . . Former Spurs and Watford winger Bobby Cook died aged 72.

6 March 1999 . . . Former Manchester United and Stoke goalscorer Dennis Viollet, English international, died aged 65.

7 March 1919 . . . Thomas Allsopp, the only man to play cricket for Leicestershire and Norfolk, and football for Leicester and Norwich, died aged 38.

7 March 1947 . . . Former Manchester City and Norwich centre half Sid Scott died aged 55.

7 March 1985 . . . Keeper for Norwich and Torquay Derek Davis died aged 62.

7 March 1990 . . . Former Everton keeper Albert Dunlop died aged 57.

8 March 1976 . . . Former Swindon, Bolton and Spurs keeper Bill Hinton died aged 80.

8 March 1988 . . . Former England international Frank Osborne, born in South Africa but an England international, who played for Spurs and Southampton before becoming Fulham manager, died aged 91.

9 March 1976 . . . Former Doncaster and Norwich centre half John Scott died aged 70.

10 March 1995 . . . Former Swindon and Hull winger Charles Manning died in his 88th year.

11 March 1995 . . . Former Man U, Northampton and Brentford keeper Ignatius 'Sonny' Feehan died aged 68.

11 March 1999 . . . Third Lanark and Stranraer striker John 'Jack' Jones died aged 82.

12 March 1968 . . . Ray Bennion, who won ten Welsh caps and played over 300 times for Man U, died aged 71.

12 March 1973 . . . Former Spurs captain and half back Arthur Grimsdell died aged 78.

12 March 1991 . . . Former Port Vale and Norwich right half William Cleary died aged 59.

13 March 1997 . . . Former Bradford PA and Middlesbrough winger Geoff Walker died aged 70.

14 March 1986 . . . Former Blackburn and England winger Jack Bruton died aged 82.

14 March 1996 . . . Former Mansfield Town winger turned full back Sam Chessell died aged 74.

14 March 1997 . . . Former Chesterfield, Portsmouth and Exeter winger Gordon Dale died aged 71.

14 March 1998 . . . England international, member of Chelsea championship winning side Peter Sillett died aged 65.

15 March 1939 . . . No doubt hurricane-like in his play, Alex Higgins, inside forward for Kilmarnock – for whom he

was scheduled to play in the Scottish Cup Final on the day his father died – Notts Forest and Newcastle, died aged 53.

15 March 1964 . . . Former Norwich, Luton, Brentford half back William Bushell died aged 82.

15 March 1981 . . . Joseph Brain, pigeon fancier and former centre forward for Sunderland, Norwich, Barrow, Preston and Swansea – where he was top scorer for two seasons – as well as Bristol City, died aged 71.

15 March 1990 . . . Football League President 1966–74 Len Shipman died aged 87.

15 March 2000 . . . Former Swindon and Colchester midfielder Ray Bunkell died aged 50.

16 March 1999 . . . Harry Colville, Falkirk, Raith and Dunfermline centre half who managed Cowdenbeath, died aged 74.

16 March 1999 . . . Former Oldham and St Johnstone forward John Liddell died aged 65.

17 March 1956 . . . Former Chelsea player Charles Freeman died.

17 March 1999 . . . Former Morton and Southampton inside forward Tom McGarrity died aged 76.

19 March 1949 . . . Former Millwall, Clapton Orient and Accrington Stanley player Bob Duffus died aged 58 – whilst watching a football match.

19 March 1977 . . . Former Chelsea player Peter Houseman and his wife Sally died in a car crash, only hours after he had played for Oxford United.

19 March 1997 . . . Former Fulham full back Henry Freeman died aged 78.

19 March 1998 . . . Former Raith, Doncaster and Wrexham keeper Archie Ferguson died aged 79.

19 March 1998 . . . After playing 247 League games for Portsmouth and 247 League games for Newcastle; and, as manager, taking Cardiff to the semi final of the European Cup Winners' Cup, Jimmy Scoular died aged 73.

20 March 1990 . . . The original 'man in black', great USSR keeper Lev Yashin, 78 caps and the first sportsman to become a Hero of Socialist Labour, died aged 60.

21 March 1979 . . . Former Norwich keeper Leslie Allmam, who once almost caused a riot by continuously kicking the ball off the penalty spot in protest at the decision – then saved the kick – died aged 76.

22 March 1930 . . . First manager – in all but name – of Liverpool John McKenna died aged 82.

23 March 1947 . . . Former Liverpool, Oldham and Manchester City manager David Ashworth died aged 79.

23 March 1986 . . . Former Hibs and Northern Ireland player Jack Jones died aged 78.

23 March 1995 . . . Scottish international Davie Cooper, who played for Rangers and Motherwell, collapsed and died aged 39, whilst coaching youngsters for a TV programme. Even Celtic fans left tributes, along with thousands of others from his two clubs.

24 March 1968 . . . Former Norwich left half Thomas Henry Hopewell died aged 71.

24 March 1976 . . . Former Norwich and Peterborough winger Alf Ford died aged 74.

24 March 2000 . . . George Kirby, who liked to get about a bit, died aged 76. He managed in England – Halifax, Watford – Kuwait, Iceland, Indonesia and Saudi Arabia.

25 March 1954 . . . William Jackson, who played 64 times scoring fourteen goals for Man U – then Newton Heath – at the turn of the century, before being signed by Barrow, died aged 78.

25 March 1957 . . . Former Norwich, Notts County and Chesterfield left half Fred Bemment died aged 72.

25 March 1998 . . . Former East Fife, Hearts and Brechin defender Jimmy Philip died aged 84.

26 March 1979 . . . Former Norwich and Exeter full back William 'Ginger' Smith died aged 73.

27 March 2001 . . . *The Times* reported that the late Dixie Dean's 1933 FA Cup winner's medal had been bought by his former club Everton at auction for £18,212.

28 March 1972 . . . Bobby Steel, one of three brothers (Alex and Danny were the others) to play for Spurs, who made 230 appearances for them before becoming a referee and resuming playing with Gillingham, died aged 84.

28 March 1974 . . . Former Charlton, Doncaster, Southport, Hartlepool, Norwich and Reading centre forward Les Owens died aged 54.

29 March 1959 . . . Former WBA and England international Billy G Richardson collapsed and died during a charity match at Perry Barr, Birmingham, aged 49.

29 March 1960 . . . 1908 FA Cup winning keeper for Wolves Tommy Lunn, who later played for Spurs and Stockport, died aged 66.

30 March 1943 . . . Luton Town player Sergeant Charlie Clark died of war wounds.

30 March 2001 . . . It was reported that whilst attending the funeral of a friend, former Liverpool and England player Emlyn Hughes was burgled, losing 'whisky bottles that I was given for being manager of the month at Rotherham – they are worth a fortune to me.'

31 March 2001 . . . Former England, Arsenal and Leeds midfielder David Rocastle died of cancer, aged 33.

1 April 1984 . . . Former Wolves, Norwich and Northampton left half Tom Smalley died aged 71.

1 April 1987 . . . Flamboyant midfielder Trevor Hockey – who made a record called 'Happy Cos I'm Blue' when with Birmingham, and also played for Forest, Villa, Norwich, Bradford and was a Welsh international, sent off against Poland – died in his kit, after playing in an indoor five-a-side game, aged 44.

1 April 1988 . . . Former Blackburn, Stoke and Norwich centre half Tom Williamson was killed by a cigarette – he fell asleep whilst smoking and died by carbon monoxide poisoning at the age of 87.

1 April 1995 . . . FA Cup winner with WBA and England international, inside forward Johnny Nicholls died aged 63.

1 April 1996 . . . Morton, Torquay, Falkirk and Stenhousemuir keeper Archie McFeat died aged 72.

2 April 1979 . . . Former England international winger Samuel Austin, of Norwich and Manchester City, died aged 78.

2 April 1984 . . . Former Chelsea player Frank Rawlinson Mitchell died.

2 April 1998 . . . Ronnie Dix, youngest scorer of Football League when on target for Bristol Rovers against Norwich in March 1928 aged 15 years and 180 days. He went on to play for England and died on this day, aged 85.

3 April 2001 . . . TalkSport Radio station announced that university researchers were endeavouring to acquire 500 brains of deceased footballers in order to research the possibly adverse effects of heading a football regularly over a lengthy period of time.

4 April 1949 . . . Former Chelsea player Sidney Bishop died.

4 April 1959 . . . With seventeen caps for England and 265 appearances for Birmingham to his credit, full back Jeff Hall contracted polio and died aged just 29. He was commemorated by the Jeff Hall memorial scoreboard and clock at the City End of St Andrew's.

4 April 1982 . . . Former WBA half back James Edwards, who had 'legs that would comfortably have supported an oil rig', died aged 76.

5 April 1902 . . . Twenty-six people died and 587 were injured during a Scotland v England match at Ibrox when terracing collapsed.

6 April 1938 . . . Fred Erentz, whose brother Harry also played for them, played over 300 times for Newton Heath, and died aged 67.

6 April 1940 . . . The first player signed on professional terms by Spurs, Jock Montgomery, died aged 63.

6 April 1949 . . . Pitman-turned-footballer with Motherwell, Preston and Spurs, full back Sandy 'Terrible' Tait died in his 77th year.

6 April 1971 . . . Former Preston, Lincoln and Norwich inside right Joseph Hetherington died aged 78.

6 April 1990 . . . Former Man City inside forward and Irish manager Peter Doherty died aged 77.

6 April 1997 . . . Five spectators were crushed to death at Nigeria's national stadium in Lagos when not enough gates were opened as the 40,000 crowd left after a 2–1 World Cup win over Guinea.

8 April 1935 . . . Fulham full back Sonny Gibbon was killed in a motor-cycle accident whilst still actively playing for the club.

8 April 1944 . . . Former Liverpool, Derby, and Fulham winger Hugh McQueen died aged 76.

8 April 1983 . . . Former Norwich winger William Cousins died aged 80.

9 April 1966 . . . Former Sheffield Wednesday and Norwich centre half Barry Butler died from car crash injuries, aged 31.

9 April 1985 . . . Ernie Taylor, the first player signed by Man U – from Sunderland – after the Munich air crash, died aged 59.

9 April 1995 . . . Former winner of thirteen England caps, Sunderland inside forward Raich Carter died aged 80.

10 April 1972 . . . Former Port Vale, Norwich, Watford and Mansfield keeper Ormond Jones died aged 61.

10 April 1994 . . . Former Preston, Bristol City and Northampton forward Archie Garrett died aged 74.

11 April 1995 . . . Former Sheffield United and Blackburn full back Mick Heaton died aged 48 in a road accident.

13 April 1959 . . . Former QPR, Notts County, Chelsea, Spurs, Leicester and Norwich forward Percy Humphreys died aged 78.

14 April 1997 . . . Former Wigan, Cardiff, Middlesbrough, Preston and Bradford City defender Jack Jennings died aged 94.

14 April 2000 . . . Wilf Mannion, who won 26 caps and played 341 League games – scoring 99 goals – for Middlesbrough, and was known as the Golden Boy because of his blond hair, died aged 81.

15 April 1952 . . . Former Spurs, Dundee and Manchester City player and Huddersfield manager John Chaplin died aged 69.

15 April 1981 . . . Former Norwich winger Sid Jones died aged 59.

15 April 1989 . . . Hillsborough tragedy in which 95 people died.

17 April 1998 . . . Fulham stalwart, Republic of Ireland international wing half Joseph 'Robin' Lawler died aged 73.

18 April 1996 . . . United Arab Emirates supporter and bigwig Sheikh Mohammed bin Khalid al-Qassimi died in Glasgow, aged 28, from complications, having been hit by a firework whilst watching UAE play Dubai on 22 March.

19 April 1958 . . . Billy Meredith of Manchester City, Man U and Wales, who was still playing at 49 and was once suspended for allegedly offering bribes during a game, died aged 83.

20 April 1935 . . . A player and then manager at Spurs, John Cameron died aged 63.

21 April 1995 . . . Toymaker and Bradford chairman Stafford Heginbotham died aged 61.

22 April 1989 . . . Every League match kicked off at 3.06pm to mark the time at which the Liverpool-Forest Cup semi final was abandoned at Hillsborough the previous week. A minute's silence was also observed.

22 April 1991 . . . Former Norwich and Colchester left half John Bell died aged 51.

22 April 1998 . . . Norman Coupe joined Carlisle as full back after taking part in the D-Day landings and later transferring to Rochdale. He died aged 73.

23 April 1932 . . . Sheffield United's long-serving secretary-manager John Nicholson was knocked down and killed at the station where the side were preparing for their trip to Aston villa for a League match – which duly went ahead, with a distracted United losing 5–0.

23 April 1977 . . . Former Newcastle, Barnsley, Brighton and Norwich right half Matt McNeil died aged 49.

23 April 1986 . . . Spurs footballer and England cricketer Bill Eldrich died aged 70.

23 April 1997 . . . Former Middlesex and England cricketer, and FA Cup winner with Arsenal, Denis Compton died aged 78.

23 April 1997 . . . Former Coventry and Leicester winger Brian Alderson died in Atlanta, US, aged 46.

23 April 1999 . . . Brighton, Bournemouth and Palace winger Walter Hanlon died aged 79.

24 April 1962 . . . Edward Barkas, a centre forward for several clubs including Norwich, Huddersfield, Birmingham and Chelsea, died aged 60.

24 April 1969 . . . Former Bournemouth and Norwich full back Harry Wingham died aged 73.

24 April 1996 . . . Former York City wing half Ron Spence – 281 League games 1948–60 – died aged 72.

24 April 1997 . . . Former Port Vale and Halifax defender William Allsop died aged 85.

25 April 1980 . . . Former Norwich full back Gordon Hepple died aged 54.

25 April 1997 . . . Former Raith, Sheffield United, Dundee, Hamilton, Falkirk, Forfar and Stirling winger Frank Joyner died aged 78.

26 April 1946 . . . Billy Porter, who played for Oldham and Man U before becoming player-manager at Hyde United, died suddenly, aged 40.

26 April 2001 Former BBC radio football commentator and writer, Bryon Butler died aged 66.

28 April 1999 . . . Legendary England World Cup winning manager and England international Sir Alf Ramsey died aged 78.

29 April 1931 . . . Former Spurs and Third Lanark player Danny Steel died aged 46.

29 April 1999 . . . Former Spurs and West Ham striker Les Bennett died aged 81.

29 April 2001 . . . Seven people were reported dead after a riot broke out at a match between two of Congo's top sides, Mazembe and Lupopo.

30 April 1933 . . . Newcastle player turned trainer Wilf Lawson died aged 48, in a road accident.

30 April 1964 . . . Former Arsenal, Spurs and Norwich keeper Ernest Williamson, who won two England caps, died aged 73.

30 April 1993 . . . Former Manchester City, Arsenal and Charlton defender Tommy Caton died aged 30.

1 May 1996 . . . Eric Houghton, who served Aston Villa for 50 years as player, manager and director, died aged 85. Scored 72 of 79 penalty kicks. Won five England caps. Managed Villa to win the FA Cup in 1957.

2 May 1996 . . . The Manchester City chairman whom fans loved to hate and hated to love, strand-haired Peter Swales died aged 63.

3 May 1914 . . . Five days after Rangers staged a benefit game for their trainer of seventeen years, Jimmy Wilson, he died.

3 May 1949 . . . Former Spurs player and Test Match umpire Fanny Walden died aged 61.

4 May 1955 . . . Former Norwich and Scunthorpe left half James Broadhead died aged 60.

5 May 1962 . . . Former Sheffield Wednesday and Norwich right back George Gray 'died an unfortunate death in his kitchen' aged 66, according to the enigmatic entry in Mike Davage's *Glorious Canaries*. You mean there is such a thing as a 'fortunate death'?

5 May 1992 . . . Fifteen spectators died when a temporary stand erected in Bastia, Corsica, for a French Cup semi-final collapsed.

5 May 1999 . . . Sir Stanley Matthews died aged 84.

6 May 1962 . . . Former Sunderland, Portsmouth and Norwich centre half Isaac Martin died aged 72.

6 May 2001 . . . Fighting among fans at an ASEC Abidjan-African Sports game in Ivory Coast led to one death.

8 May 1965 . . . Harry Hardinge, who played both football and cricket for England, died.

8 May 1984 . . . A young Spurs fan was shot dead in a Brussels bar the day before the Spurs v Anderlecht UEFA Cup Final first leg.

8 May 1994 . . . The first player filmed by TV signing a contract, when he moved from Brentford to West Ham in 1955, Billy Dare died aged 67.

8 May 1998 . . . Former Newcastle, Lincoln, Workington, Chesterfield, Bradford forward Ernie Whittle died aged 72.

9 May 1978 . . . Former Chelsea player Leonard Hector Allum died.

9 May 2001 . . . Over one hundred and twenty fans died after a stampede at a match between Ghana's top sides, Hearts of Oak and Asante Kotoko.

10 May 1968 . . . The – for professional footballers – uniquely named Cromwell Bradley, a winger for Norwich and

Sheffield Wednesday, also known as Cecil, died aged 63.

10 May 1997 . . . Ivor Allchurch, 68 Welsh caps and author of a book boasting a blank chapter representing the average director's knowledge of the game, died aged 67.

11 May 1996 . . . Former Lincoln and Accrington player Jimmy Grummett died aged 77.

12 May 2001 . . . Brazilian midfielder, Didi, a member of their 1958 and 62 World Cup winning sides, died aged 71.

13 May 1971 . . . FA Cup winner with Spurs, Charlie Walters, who also played for Fulham and Mansfield, died aged 74.

13 May 1974 . . . Neil McBain who, in 1947, became the oldest player to appear in a Football League match when, as boss, he picked himself in goal for New Brighton, died aged 79.

13 May 1989 . . . Newcastle fans held a spontaneous minute's silence after losing at home 0–2 to Man U, in memory of Darren, an otherwise anonymous fan who was said to have been killed at a game in London earlier that season, in a fight with rugby league fans. An urban myth, perhaps?

13 May 1994 . . . Sunderland, Derby and Exeter centre half Ken Oliver died aged 69.

14 May 1949 . . . Italian champions Torino were wiped out

when 28 died in the plane taking them back from a Benfica game, which crashed at Superga, near Turin.

14 May 1994 . . . Workington inside forward Arnold Timmins died aged 54.

15 May 2001 . . . Scotland international and member of 1967 Celtic European Cup winning side, midfielder Bobby Murdoch, died aged 56.

18 May 1948 . . . Former Norwich player John Allen died aged 57.

18 May 1998 . . . Former East Fife, Clyde and Arbroath inside forward Ian Stewart died in his 58th year.

19 May 1994 . . . A replacement at Stoke for Stanley Matthews when he left for Blackpool, winger John Malkin died aged 68.

20 May 1964 . . . Former Norwich and Grimsby inside forward Langford Baker died aged 85.

21 May 1940 . . . Twice top scorer for Reading and three times for Spurs, for whom he later became manager, Billy Minter died aged 52.

21 May 1967 . . . Keeper for Villa and Spurs' manager for Cardiff, Norwich, Palace and Exeter, Cyril Spiers died aged 65.

22 May 1967 . . . Former Notts County, Spurs and England player Willie Hall died aged 55.

22 May 1979 . . . Former Portsmouth, Bournemouth, Port Vale, Preston and Norwich winger John Friar died aged 67.

22 May 1981 . . . Former Reading, Southampton, Norwich, Rochdale and Exeter right half Alexander Christie died aged 84.

22 May 1990 . . . Former Norwich, Watford, Exeter and Newport forward Peter Gordon died, the day after his 58th birthday.

22 May 1991 . . . The first player to score an FA Cup Final hat-trick, Blackpool and England – 25 caps – forward Stan Mortensen died aged 69.

22 May 1998 . . . Former Swindon half back Fred Thompson died aged 60.

23 May 1997 . . . Former Manchester City and Bristol City player John Hampshire died aged 83.

23 May 1997 . . . Former Notts County half back Harry Adamson died aged 72.

23 May 1999 . . . Ref with 73 internationals to his credit, including 1950 World Cup games, Arthur Ellis died aged 84.

24 May 1964 . . . Three hundred and eighteen people died when a crowd riot broke out at National Stadium in Lima, over a disallowed goal in the Olympic qualifying match between home side Peru and Argentina.

24 May 1995 . . . Huddersfield Town triple First Division title winner and winger Joe Walter died in his 99th year.

25 May 1942 . . . Former Norwich, Tranmere, Palace and Mansfield forward Reginald Cooper died aged 40.

25 May 1995 . . . Southampton striker Derek Reeves, who set the Third Division post-war goalscoring record with 39 in 46 games in 1959–60, died aged 60.

26 May 1985 . . . Ten people died during a crowd panic at the Olympic Stadium, Mexico City, where the Cup Final was taking place.

27 May 1940 . . . At just 25 years old, Newcastle's Stan Docking died of a heart attack whilst on leave from the RAF.

27 May 1942 . . . FA Cup winner with Bury, James 'Punch' McEwen, a full back, also played for Luton, and Norwich – where he became manager – and later became assistant trainer at Arsenal. He died on this day aged 69.

29 May 1985 . . . Thirty-nine people – mainly Italians – died when fighting broke out and a wall collapsed at the Heysel

Stadium in Brussels, where Liverpool and Juventus were playing the European Cup Final.

29 May 1995 . . . Ted Drake died aged 82. He played for Southampton and Arsenal, where he scored 42 goals in 41 games in his first full season. He also won five England caps and, as Chelsea manager, sold Jimmy Greaves to AC Milan.

30 May 1993 . . . The youngest man to play in all four Divisions, Mel Rees of Cardiff, WBA, Watford and Sheffield United, died of cancer, aged 26.

31 May 1995 . . . Former Sunderland, Cardiff and Darlington defender Tim Gilbert died aged 36.

31 May 1995 . . . Scorer of the goal which beat Manchester Utd in the 1976 FA Cup Final, Southampton's Bobby Stokes died aged 43.

1 June 1998 . . . Former Bristol City and Torquay – 204 goals in 358 League games – player Ronald 'Sammy' Collins died aged 75.

2 June 1943 . . . Barnsley and Portsmouth winger George Bullock, a naval rating, died in a road accident.

2 June 1962 . . . Former Norwich, Millwall and Charlton forward Johnny Summers died aged 34, of leukaemia.

2 June 1978 . . . Ernest Vincent of Southport, Man U – who bought him in 1932 for £1,000 – QPR and Doncaster, died aged 70.

3 June 1953 . . . Spectacularly mustachioed former Norwich custodian William Cooks exited, aged 79.

3 June 1968 . . . Former England international and Spurs and Forest half-back Wally Alsford died in his 58th year.

3 June 1997 . . . Former Southport wing half Tommy Holmes died aged 95.

4 June 1953 . . . Former Wolves and Norwich keeper Lewis Botto died aged 54.

4 June 1973 . . . Former Leicester and Norwich forward John Parker died aged 77.

5 June 1971 . . . Former Liverpool player Kevin Baron died aged 44.

5 June 1985 . . . Frank Hodges of Birmingham, Man U and Crewe, died aged 96.

6 June 1925 . . . Former Spurs keeper Bill Jacques died.

6 June 1984 . . . Former Hibs, Luton, Clapton Orient,

Brighton, Walsall, Norwich, Brentford and Swindon inside forward Norman Thomson died aged 83.

6 June 1994 . . . Former Carlisle, Newcastle, Manchester United and QPR winger, Jackie Cape died aged 83.

6 June 1994 . . . A bomber pilot who won the DFC for heroism during the Second World War, Ken Wright, striker for West Ham, died on the 50th anniversary of D-Day.

7 June 1989 . . . Former Huddersfield and Man U (92 appearances) player George Roughton, who then became player-manager at Exeter, died aged 79.

8 June 2001 . . . Former Arsenal, Southampton forward Don Roper died aged 78.

9 June 1965 . . . Harold Hardman, who spent his career as an amateur but won the FA Cup with Everton in 1906, died aged 83.

9 June 1994 . . . Former Hearts, Morton and Stirling keeper Gordon Millar died in his 46th year.

9 June 2001 . . . Ronnie Allen, who scored twice when WBA won the 1954 FA Cup Final and who went on to manage Albion, Walsall, Wolves, Athletic Bilbao, Sporting Lisbon and Saudi Arabia, died aged 72.

10 June 1998 . . . Regular hitman for Halifax, Portsmouth, Aldershot, Barnsley and York James Griffiths died aged 84.

11 June 1916 . . . Dick Pegg – who scored the first League match hat-trick scored for Man U (against Bradford City on 26 September 1903) – died aged 38.

12 June 1965 . . . Former Chelsea player John Jackson died in Canada.

13 June 1948 . . . Prolific scorer James Bauchop, who netted on his debuts for Celtic, Norwich, Palace, Derby, Spurs, Bradford and Lincoln, died aged 62.

14 June 1968 . . . Former Spurs and Clapton Orient inside forward and England international Bert Bliss died aged 78.

14 June 1975 . . . Former Newcastle player Joe Richardson died aged 66.

14 June 1996 . . . Former Arbroath full back Bobby Clark died aged 67.

14 June 1996 . . . Former Bristol Rovers, Mansfield and Brentford player Roger Frude died aged 76.

16 June 1981 . . . Former Chelsea player William Marshall Hughes died.

16 June 1996 . . . Former Manchester United centre half – 352 League games – Allenby Chilton, who won two England caps, died aged 77.

19 June 1969 . . . Former Spurs player George Forman, who boxed clever to play for West Ham and Spurs, died aged 55.

19 June 1996 . . . Former Newcastle player and Middlesbrough manager Bob Dennison died aged 84.

20 June 1973 . . . Former Spurs and Bristol Rovers keeper Joe Nicholls died aged 68.

20 June 1981 . . . Former Man U Second Division title winner (1935–6) player George Vose died aged 69.

20 June 1987 . . . Former Newcastle striker Andy Donaldson died aged 62.

21 June 1998 . . . Preston skipper when they won the 1938 FA Cup Final, Tom Smith died aged 88.

22 June 1919 . . . Former Manchester City player Frank 'Tabby' Booth died from injuries sustained during the First World War.

22 June 1956 . . . Former Norwich, Birmingham and Notts County centre forward Percy Gooch died aged 73.

22 June 1996 . . . Spurs, Cardiff, Gillingham and Torquay keeper Terry Lee died aged 43.

22 June 1997 . . . Former Manchester City, Oldham and Bury winger Jimmy Munro died aged 71.

23 June 1917 . . . Manchester City and Birmingham player, James Conlin, was killed in Flanders whilst serving in the Highland Light Infantry.

23 June 1977 . . . Former Norwich, Charlton, Mansfield and Walsall inside right Archibald Chappell died aged 66.

23 June 1996 . . . One-club-man Gordon Williams, 127 League appearances as wing half for Swindon, died aged 71.

24 June 1973 . . . A scorer in all four Divisions, Robert Dennison of Norwich, Brighton, Manchester City, Clapton Orient and Chesterfield, died aged 72, having scored Norwich's first League hat-trick.

24 June 1976 . . . Former Newcastle player Harry Bedford died aged 76.

24 June 1994 . . . Former Middlesbrough and Darlington full back Syd Jarvis died in his 89th year.

25 June 1921 . . . 1899 FA Cup finalist for Derby, Tommy Arkesden, died aged 42.

25 June 1940 . . . Liverpool right back Tommy Cooper died in a motorcycle accident, aged 36, whilst serving in the Military Police.

25 June 1997 . . . Former Hearts, Ipswich and Colchester forward, Bobby Blackwood died aged 62.

26 June 1997 . . . Former Mansfield stalwart defender Don Bradley died aged 72.

27 June 1958 . . . Former Norwich defender Reg Desborough died aged 78.

28 June 1941 . . . Bert Middlemiss, who scored 51 goals in 248 League appearances for Spurs, died aged 52.

28 June 1986 . . . Former Norwich winger Sid Plunkett died aged 65.

28 June 1997 . . . Former Spurs and Crystal Palace player Charlie Rundle died aged 74.

28 June 1998 . . . Former Manchester United and England forward Jack Rowley, later Plymouth player-manager, died aged 77.

29 June 1949 . . . A Liverpool stalwart in their title-winning teams of 1922 and 1923, Harry Chambers died aged 53.

29 June 1972 . . . Former Third Lanark, Airdrie, St Mirren and Norwich keeper Bill O'Hagan died aged 81.

29 June 1998 . . . Former Celtic player, Roy Milne, who won international honours for the USA, died aged 77.

30 June 1990 . . . Former Villa player Brian Tiler died in a car crash in Italy which left Harry Redknapp seriously injured. Tiler played 106 League matches for Villa and was Bournemouth chief executive.

30 June 2001 . . . Former Liverpool manager Joe Fagan – who took the club to a European Cup, League title and League Cup treble, in 1983–4, died aged 80.

1 July 1966 . . . Ten days before the World Cup began, Joe Mears, chairman of the FA, died. Four pages had to be added at the last moment to the tournament's commemorative programme in tribute.

2 July 1994 . . . Colombian World Cup defender Andres Escobar, scorer of an own goal against the USA in the World Cup, was mysteriously gunned down, aged 26.

2 July 1997 . . . Former Stoke and Derby forward George Antonio died aged 82.

3 July 1972 . . . His career ended when he was suspended for betting on matches in March 1924, but Norwich left back Bennie Smith died aged 80 on this day.

3 July 1996 . . . Scorer of the fastest goal in Bristol Rovers' history – after eight seconds against Aldershot – striker Vic Lambden died aged 70.

3 July 1997 . . . Former Spurs and Swansea keeper Percy Hooper died aged 82.

3 July 1998 . . . Scottish League Cup winner with Dundee, Alf Boyd, who managed Durban City in South Africa, died aged 77.

4 July 1956 . . . Former pitman turned Spurs player – 92 goals in 252 League appearances – Eugene O'Callaghan died aged 49.

4 July 1980 . . . Former Norwich right back Denis Morgan died aged 54, after developing gangrene in his leg.

5 July 1987 . . . Former Newcastle player Bobby Ancell died aged 76.

5 July 1987 . . . Former Newcastle player Jack Little died aged 83.

5 July 1997 . . . Former Sheffield United and Hull half back John Sheen died aged 76.

6 July 1984 . . . Former Newcastle player Lawrie Crown died aged 86.

7 July 1947 . . . Bolton keeper in the 1894 FA Cup final in which they lost 4–1 to Notts County, John Sutcliffe died aged 79.

7 July 1974 . . . Former Chelsea player George Barber died.

7 July 1996 . . . Former Cowdenbeath striker Billy Bostock died aged 52.

8 July 2001 . . . 1987 FA Cup Final ref, Neil Midgley, died aged 58.

9 July 1918 . . . Former Sheffield Wednesday and Spurs defender William Findlay Weir was killed in action whilst serving with the army in France, aged 29.

10 July 1988 . . . Former Norwich striker Alf Ackerman died in his native South Africa, aged 59.

13 July 1929 . . . Former Hearts and Spurs player Tom Collins, who lost an arm and a leg during the First World War, died aged 47.

13 July 1941 . . . Splendidly named Welsh international, Willy Lot Jones of Manchester City, died aged 59.

13 July 1961 . . . Clarence Norman Wharton, former keeper who played in all four Divisions for sides including Preston, Barrow, Sheffield United, Norwich and York, died aged 57.

14 July 1918 . . . Former Norwich, Luton, Peterborough and Millwall inside forward George Porter died aged 31, from war wounds.

15 July 1966 . . . Jimmy Seed died aged 71. He played for Sunderland and Spurs, who won the 1921 FA Cup; Sheffield Wednesday, winning two consecutive championships. He became manager at Clapton Orient and Charlton, where he again won the FA Cup; and then Bristol City and Millwall.

15 July 1978 . . . Former Chelsea player George Robert Mills died.

15 July 1963 . . . Former Norwich, Grimsby and Accrington half back Richard Field died aged 71.

15 July 1989 . . . The second black player to win a full England cap, Laurie Cunningham, was killed in a car crash.

16 July 1957 . . . Former Stoke, Sheffield United – with whom he won the 1915 FA Cup – and Norwich full back Albert 'Hair Pin' (don't ask me!) Sturgess died aged 74.

16 July 1990 . . . Former Real Madrid player and manager, Miguel Munoz, died aged 68.

17 July 1977 . . . Arthur Jepson, Nottinghamshire cricketer, Test umpire and keeper for Port Vale, Stoke and Lincoln, died aged 72.

18 July 1986 . . . Great football administrator Sir Stanley Rous, goalkeeper, referee, FA secretary and FIFA president, died aged 91.

19 July 1947 . . . Dundee, Oldham, Newton Heath and Spurs defender Harry 'Tiger' Erentz died aged 72.

19 July 1989 . . . Former Sunderland, Blackpool, Norwich wing half and Shrewsbury player-manager Stan Ramsay died aged 84.

20 July 1969 . . . Former Norwich wing half Joe Jobling died aged 62.

20 July 1996 . . . Former Blackburn and Stockport winger Chris Anderson died aged 67.

20 July 1994 . . . Former Rangers, Dundee and Arbroath player Andy Penman – one Scottish cap – died aged 51.

21 July 1964 . . . Spurs Scottish international John White was killed by lightning while sheltering under a tree during a thunderstorm on Crews Hill Golf Course at Enfield, aged 27.

21 July 1988 . . . Former Man U, Villa, Northampton and Brighton player Frank Brett died aged 89.

22 July 1959 . . . Prolific Blackburn, Preston and Spurs striker Ted Harper died aged 57.

22 July 1976 . . . Welsh international Willie Evans, who played almost all of his senior career with Spurs as an inside forward and winger, died aged 63.

23 July 1941 . . . They came to bury Caesar Jenkyns, 74, former Welsh international.

24 July 1996 . . . The first man to manage Rangers twice, Jock (John Martin Bokas) Wallace, died aged 60. He was also a former keeper with Workington.

25 July 2001 . . . Bertie Felstead, last survivor of First World War 1915 Xmas Day truce when British and German troops played football together, leaving their trenches in Laventie, N. France, died aged 106.

27 July 1964 . . . Former Chelsea goalkeeper Peter McKenna died.

27 July 1996 . . . Winner of four Welsh caps, inside forward William Rees died aged 72.

28 July 1952 . . . Former Spurs player and Northampton manager, Walter Bull died aged 78.

28 July 1963 . . . Former Welsh international Albert Jones, full back for Swindon, Forest, Notts County and Norwich, died aged 80.

28 July 1994 . . . Arthur Holt, Southampton and Man U inside forward – who also played cricket for Hampshire – died aged 83.

28 July 2001 . . . The Daily Mirror reported: "Earlier this month a Bangkok Liverpool fan flung himself from a tower block because he couldn't get his hands on a ticket for their game against the Thai national side."

29 July 1969 . . . Former Norwich and Southampton winger Charles Curtin died aged 79.

31 July 1926 . . . Former Rangers player and director, John McPherson died.

31 July 1952 . . . Former Bolton, Plymouth, Man U, Burnley and Bristol City forward Jack Picken died aged 72.

31 July 1960 . . . The oldest player to turn out for Spurs in a League game, Jimmy Cantrell, who was 40 at the time, and who later became a golf professional, died aged 78.

31 July 1986 . . . Peter McCoy, Newcastle and Norwich full back, died on his 63rd birthday.

3 August 1971 . . . Former Swansea, Darlington, Blackpool and Norwich inside right John Middleton died aged 61.

5 August 1983 . . . Former Chelsea player Alexander Cheyne died.

5 August 1994 . . . Former Leeds, Newcastle and Birmingham midfielder Terry Hibbitt died aged 46.

5 August 2001 . . . Portsmouth keeper Aaron Flahavon, 25, was killed in a car crash. He had twice collapsed during matches, and Pompey withdrew his Number 1 jersey for the season.

6 August 1953 . . . Welsh international and former Notts County, Swansea, Cardiff and Spurs winger William Davies died aged 53.

6 August 1976 . . . Fred Channell, a Spurs full back forced to retire through injury at just 26, died aged 66.

6 August 1976 . . . Former Northampton, Norwich and Barrow full back Fred Ferrari died aged 75.

6 August 1993 . . . Former Derby, Norwich and Doncaster keeper Ken Oxford died aged 63.

7 August 1939 . . . Founder and Chairman of the Players' Union, Charlie Roberts of Man U and Oldham, died aged 56.

7 August 1973 . . . Freddie Cox, who won the FA Cup and League championship with Arsenal and later managed Bournemouth – twice – Portsmouth and Gillingham, died aged 52.

7 August 1984 . . . Former Hartlepool and Northampton inside forward John Hewitt died aged 73.

8 August 1998 . . . Former Dundee Utd, Norwich and Dunfermline winger Maurice Milne died aged 65.

9 August 1961 . . . The first Brazilian-born player in the Football League, former Norwich and Notts County winger Edward Laxton, died aged 64.

9 August 1973 . . . Former Queens Park; Rangers; Preston; Newcastle and Norwich player William Aitken died aged 79.

9 August 1990 . . . Former England manager for seven games; Everton and Arsenal player and wartime international, later Sheffield United, Villa and Manchester City boss Joe Mercer OBE died on his 76th birthday.

9 August 1991 . . . Former Sunderland, Lincoln, Bradford City and Norwich winger Frank Pegg died aged 89.

11 August 1971 . . . Former Plymouth defender James Dickinson, who was engaged in anti-submarine activities in the First World War, died aged 71.

12 August 1994 . . . Former Charlton forward Ron White died aged 62.

13 August 1979 . . . Former Huddersfield, Norwich, Luton and York winger Jacky Slicer died aged 76.

13 August 1988 . . . Former Ipswich and Norwich keeper – who played in the first fixture at Carrow Road – Harold Dukes died aged 76.

13 August 2001 . . . Reports revealed that 2 players died when lightning struck in Guatemala as Deportivo Chiquimulilla and Pueblo Nuevo Vinas played a 3rd Division game.

14 August 1997 . . . Former Scottish international forward Charlie Fleming, also of East Fife and Sunderland, died aged 70.

16 August 1942 . . . Former Newcastle player Bob Foyers died aged 74.

18 August 1917 . . . Newcastle player James Fleming, 33, was killed in action during the First World War.

18 August 1919 . . . *Athletic News* reported that former Blackpool keeper William Fiske had been killed during the First World War, aged 34.

18 August 1924 . . . Former Chelsea player Thomas Meehan, 28, died after a bout of sleeping sickness. Two thousand people attended the funeral in Wandsworth.

18 August 1975 . . . Uncompromising Darlington and Norwich defender Thomas Halliday died aged 65.

19 August 1991 . . . Former Manchester City player and manager, Les McDowall, died aged 79.

19 August 1994 . . . Former Newcastle player Frank Houghton, a record £5,000 signing from Ballymena, died aged 68.

20 August 1936 . . . Former Newcastle player William Agnew died aged 55.

20 August 2001 . . . Death announced of Luton, Man U and West Ham Keeper Les Sealey, 43.

21 August 1979 . . . Former Leeds and Norwich full back and Bradford City manager John Milburn died aged 71.

21 August 1995 . . . Familiar-voiced Australian Leonard Martin, who had read the football results on BBC TV's *Grandstand* for 37 years, died aged 76.

22 August 1948 . . . Former Spurs player Fred Sargent died aged 36.

22 August 1981 . . . A young Newcastle supporter was accidentally killed at Roker Park, where Newcastle and Sunderland were playing a pre-season friendly.

23 August 1994 . . . Former Birmingham, Luton and Burnley defender Joe Loughran died aged 79.

23 August 1995 . . . Former Man U player – 489 games, 70 goals, Johnny Carey – capped by both Northern Ireland and the Republic of Ireland, died aged 76.

24 August 1955 . . . Former Arsenal, Reading, Gillingham, Norwich and Watford inside left Ernie North died aged 59.

25 August 1930 . . . The first Bristol Rovers keeper to score in a competitive match – in April 1910 – Peter Roney died aged 43.

25 August 1942 . . . Former Spurs, Norwich and Luton Town player Jimmy Banks died aged 49. Transfer listed by Norwich 'as he was unpopular with the other players'.

25 August 1996 . . . German international Reinhard Libuda, banned for life following a 1972 bribery scandal subsequently lifted, died.

26 August 1944 . . . Former Norwich, Middlesbrough, Reading, West Ham, Brighton, Forest, Port Vale, Stockport and Burnley inside forward Samuel Jennings – 193 goals in 375 career appearances – died aged 45.

26 August 1991 . . . Former Rangers player and assistant manager Willie Thornton died aged 71.

27 August 1938 . . . Former Newcastle player Colin Veitch, who played 322 games, died aged 57.

27 August 1984 . . . Jimmy Thompson, a friend of Lester Piggott and Gordon Richards, died at Epsom races aged 86. He was a former Millwall, Coventry, Luton, Chelsea, Norwich and Fulham player, and later discovered Jimmy Greaves and Terry Venables.

28 August 1971 . . . Former Norwich and Ipswich winger Russell Hemnell died aged 81.

28 August 1994 . . . Former Morton, Middlesbrough, Celtic, Dundee United Scottish international centre forward Neil Mochan, who ended his career with Raith, died aged 67.

28 August 2001 . . . CSKA Moscow and Ukraine keeper, Sergi Perkhun, 23, died following an on-pitch clash with Anzhi striker Budun Budanov.

29 August 1968 . . . Former Norwich left half and subsequently manager, Doug Lochhead died aged 63.

29 August 1980 . . . Former Leeds and Norwich inside left William Furness died aged 71.

29 August 1996 . . . Former Newcastle player Jimmy Gordon died aged 80.

29 August 1996 . . . Former Torquay, Birmingham, Chesterfield, Raith, Yeovil and Millwall winger Albert Bloxham died aged 90.

29 August 1998 . . . Former Mansfield defender Harry Everett died aged 77.

30 August 1944 . . . Former Norwich and Middlesbrough full back Alex Johnson died on active service on the South Arabian coast, aged 26.

30 August 1998 . . . The scorer of the penalty against Clyde which won Aberdeen the 1954–5 championship, Archie Glen died aged 69.

31 August 1960 . . . Former Chelsea player William Ferguson died.

31 August 1946 . . . Son of music hall star comedian Hyrah 'Pearly King' Travers, former Birmingham, Villa, QPR, Leicester, Man U, Swindon, Norwich and Gillingham inside right James Travers died aged 58.

31 August 1991 . . . The former Spurs and England full back who inspired the terrace chant and subsequent record 'Nice One Cyril', which reached number 14 in 1973, Cyril Knowles died aged 47.

31 August 1998 . . . Former Bury player Gareth Price died aged 28.

1 September 1956 . . . Former Norwich player Charles William Christmas – he was born 25 December, 1887 – died.

1 September 1996 . . . Former Rangers forward Jimmy Duncanson, who won three championships, three Scottish Cups and two League Cups at Ibrox, died aged 76.

1 September 1997 . . . Great Hungarian international of the fifties, Zoltan Czibor died aged 68.

1 September 2001 . . . TV commentator and Gillingham fan Brian Moore, 69, died.

2 September 1970 . . . Former Millwall, Norwich and Southend full back James Hodge died aged 79. His brother-in-law Donald McLeod of Celtic and Middlesbrough perished in the First World War.

2 September 1998 . . . Jackie Blanchflower, the brother of Danny, inside forward turned half back, had twelve Northern Ireland caps to his credit and two championship medals with Man U in 1956 and 1957. He took over in goal in the FA Cup final against Villa when keeper Ray Wood was injured. On this day he died aged 65.

2 September 2001 . . . Former Celtic and Chelsea player Bobby Evans who once sang with Bill Crosby, died aged 74..

3 September 1948 . . . Former Newcastle, Notts County, Birmingham, Port Vale, Norwich and Rochdale player John

Peart, who also became manager of the latter plus Bradford City and Fulham, died aged 59.

3 September 1994 . . . The first man to win 100 England caps and to marry Joy, one of the Beverley Sisters, Wolves centre half Billy Wright, CBE, died aged 70.

4 September 1928 . . . Former Newcastle player James Raine died aged 42.

4 September 1954 . . . Ernest Barlow, Stockport chairman 1923–54, died.

4 September 1998 . . . Former Manchester City, Bury and Millwall forward Jimmy Constantine died aged 78.

5 September 1931 . . . Celtic keeper John Thomson died following a collision with Rangers' forward Sam English.

6 September 1994 . . . Captain of West Ham when they won the Football League War Cup, and still skipper aged 41, Charlie Bicknell died aged 88.

7 September 1956 . . . C.B. Fry, who in 1902 played for Southampton in the FA Cup Final two days before scoring 82 at the Oval for London County against Surrey, died aged 84.

8 September 1990 . . . York City player David Longhurst, 35, collapsed and died from a heart attack during a match against Luton Town, being watched by his girlfriend, Vicky. A stand at the ground was re-named in his memory.

9 September 1998 . . . Derby stalwart forward Tommy Powell died aged 73.

10 September 1961 . . . Former Man U player – and, uniquely, 1908 Olympic gold medal winning cyclist – Ernie Payne died aged 76.

10 September 1985 . . . Scotland scored ten minutes from the end of their World Cup qualifier against Wales at Cardiff's Ninian Park to make the score 1–1. At the end of the match Scottish manager Jock Stein collapsed and was carried into the dressing room, where he died.

10 September 1987 . . . Former Chelsea player Benjamin Baker died.

11 September 1975 . . . Albert Frosdick, holder of the Military Medal and former Norwich outside left, died aged 81.

12 September 1961 . . . Remembered via a road near Maine Road, former Manchester City inside forward Horace Barnes died aged 70.

12 September 1996 . . . Scorer of the winning goal in the

1953–4 Scottish Cup Final for East Fife against Partick Thistle, Frank Christie, who later managed East Fife, died aged 68.

13 September 1968 . . . Frank Barson of Villa, Man U and Watford, who once received a pub as a win bonus, died aged 77. He allegedly served more suspensions than any other player.

13 September 1984 . . . Johnny Morrison, 90 goals in 134 League appearances for Spurs, died aged 73.

13 September 1995 . . . Former player and manager at Middlesbrough, Harold Sheperdson was also England's trainer when they won the 1966 World Cup Final – at which he was told to 'sit down and behave yourself' by Alf Ramsey when he showed signs of getting too excited. He died aged 76.

14 September 1946 . . . Former Brighton stalwart wing half Reg Wilkinson died aged 47, after collapsing during a match he was playing in for Norwich Electricity.

14 September 1966 . . . Former England international Villa player Frank Moss, whose son Frank also played for them, died.

15 September 1916 . . . Newcastle player Tom Rowlandson killed whilst serving in France.

15 September 1963 . . . Former Palace, Bristol City, Brentford, Norwich and Swindon inside left Cecil Blakemore died aged 65.

16 September 1939 . . . Former Chelsea player James Croal died.

16 September 1967 . . . Forty-six years a player and groundsman at Newcastle, Sandy Mutch died aged 82.

16 September 1971 . . . Former Norwich and Carlisle defender Thomas DeArr (!) Coulthard died aged 71, leaving behind no recorded explanation for that middle name.

16 September 1998 . . . Former Exeter keeper turned copper Ian Main died aged 38.

18 September 1975 . . . Former Dumbarton, Dundee, Scunthorpe, Clapton Orient, Spurs, Norwich and Stockport half back Jack Duffus died aged 74.

18 September 1981 . . . Former Norwich inside left John Scott who became, appropriately enough, a canary breeder in retirement, died aged 75.

18 September 1998 . . . Richard Whittaker, former Chelsea, Peterborough and QPR player who won a cap for the Republic, died aged 63.

19 September 1963 . . . Former Norwich winger John Duncan died aged 65.

19 September 1979 . . . Former Newcastle player Monte Wilkinson died aged 71.

19 September 1996 . . . Former Chesterfield, Spurs, Bolton and Sheffield Wednesday centre forward George Hunt, who won three England caps, died aged 86.

20 September 1946 . . . News that his brother Francis had been swept overboard from a Channel steamer arrived with Spurs player Len Duquemin on the eve of a Football Combination match against Birmingham – together with a bizarre plea from the people of Guernsey that he should nonetheless play in the match, which he did, to the approval of an 8,000 crowd.

20 September 1947 . . . Former QPR, Grimsby, Norwich, Brighton and Southend centre forward Duncan Ronaldson died aged 68.

20 September 1977 . . . Former Norwich, Portsmouth, Southend and Mansfield winger George Cooke died aged 77.

21 September 1940 . . . Former QPR, Derby, Leicester, Hull, Walsall, Norwich, Watford centre half and Irish international Michael O'Brien died aged 47.

21 September 1956 . . . Rangers manager for 34 years, William Struth died aged 81.

22 September 1961 . . . Former Norwich winger Tommy Newell died aged 82.

22 September 1999 . . . Former Scotland schoolboy and Cowdenbeath player Hamish Thomson, who won the MBE for bravery during the war, died aged 89.

23 September 1985 . . . Former Luton player and Aussie international, Phil O'Connor was killed in a car crash, aged 31.

23 September 1987 . . . Left winger for Accrington, Norwich and Lincoln, Joseph Clare died aged 77.

23 September 1990 . . . Former Norwich centre forward Peter Cleland died aged 58.

24 September 1998 . . . Former Southport, Accrington, Bristol Rovers and Bristol City and Tranmere inside forward Frank Curran died aged 81.

25 September 1991 . . . Former Norwich wing half Gordon Davies died aged 88.

25 September 1995 . . . Former manager Dave Bowen, after whom a stand at Northampton's Sixfields ground is named, died aged 67.

26 September 1981 . . . Former Celtic, Brighton and Norwich forward Patrick Gilgun died aged 79.

26 September 1989 . . . Winner of the Scottish Cup with Celtic in 1937, the FA Cup with Man U in 1948 and the Irish Cup with Derry City in 1954, Jimmy Delaney died aged 74.

27 September 1916 . . . Former Newcastle player Charles Randall died aged 34.

27 September 1999 . . . Former England inside forward, Johnny 'Budgie' Byrne, of Palace, West Ham and Fulham, who later managed Durban City in South Africa, died aged 61.

28 September 1996 . . . Holder of the record for the fastest hat-trick – in three and a half minutes for Blackpool against Fulham in 1950 – George McKnight died aged 72.

29 September 1981 . . . Legendary Liverpool manager Bill Shankly died aged 68. His most quoted quip was, of course, 'Football is not just a matter of life and death – it's much more important than that.'

30 September 1969 . . . Former Hartlepool, Norwich, QPR, York, Crewe, Aberdeen and Cardiff inside left John Duthie died aged 66.

30 September 1997 . . . Former Leicester and Mansfield winger Charlie Adam died aged 78.

30 September 1997 . . . Younger brother of England keeper Ron, Peter Springett of QPR, where he won the League Cup; and Sheffield Wednesday – where he went in a swap deal with his brother – died aged 51, after a four-year battle against crippling illness.

30 September 1998 . . . Former Northampton, Arsenal and Norwich centre half turned player-manager at Bradford PA, Laurie Brown died aged 61.

1 October 1945 . . . Former Newcastle player Bob Bennie died aged 72.

1 October 1952 . . . Former Newcastle player Peter McWilliam died aged 73.

1 October 1952 . . . Former Newcastle player Jack Fraser died aged 75.

4 October 1990 . . . Best known as Brian Clough's right hand man, Peter Taylor died aged 62.

4 October 1993 . . . Former Scotland, Man U and Coventry defender Jim Holton died at the wheel of his car, apparently from a heart attack, aged 42.

5 October 1950 . . . Former Norwich – 111 appearances – keeper, Bobby Beale died aged 66.

5 October 1955 . . . Former Everton and Manchester City striker Tommy Browell – signed initially by Hull whose officials rowed across the Tyne for his signature – died aged 62.

6 October 1985 . . . Former Scottish international and 'Wembley Wizard' Jack Harkness died aged 78.

7 October 1963 . . . Former Luton Town centre half John Fulton died aged 59.

7 October 1988 . . . Former Brighton and Norwich inside forward George Ansell died aged 78.

7 October 1994 . . . Former Reading and Palace winger Jimmy Liddle died aged 82.

7 October 2001 . . . The first Coventry player to represent England, keeper Reg Matthews, died aged 68.

8 October 1965 . . . Former Newcastle player Jimmy Nelson died aged 64.

9 October 1899 . . . Tuberculosis claimed Liverpool centre forward George Allan at the age of 24.

9 October 1994 . . . Winner of England caps either side of the war, Raich Carter, inside forward for Sunderland, Derby and Hull, manager of Leeds, Mansfield, Middlesbrough, and also Derbyshire cricketer, died aged 80.

9 October 1994 . . . Idris 'Dai' Hopkins, former Sheffield Wednesday, Palace, Brentford and Bristol City winger, who won twelve caps for Wales, died two days before his 87th birthday.

10 October 1965 . . . Former West Ham, Northampton, Norwich and Torquay inside right Leslie Robinson died aged 67.

10 October 1975 . . . Former Spurs defender Arthur Hitchens died aged 61.

10 October 1983 . . . Former Spurs inside forward Andy Duncan died aged 72.

11 October 1963 . . . Former Bradford PA, Accrington Stanley, Norwich, Sunderland and Rochdale inside left Robert Hawes, whose ability was not to be sneezed at – particularly as he invariably played clutching a handkerchief in his left hand – died aged 68.

11 October 1971 . . . After a career which ended because of a hamstring injury when he was carried off on an old door and hospitalised for fourteen weeks, former Norwich full back Bob Pointer died aged 78.

13 October 1961 . . . Former Stockport, Birmingham, Norwich, Cardiff, Doncaster, Bournemouth and Carlisle centre forward Reg Keating died aged 57.

13 October 1998 . . . Former Hearts and Scotland winger William McFarlane died aged 75.

14 October 1998 . . . Former Motherwell, Falkirk and Exeter keeper Bobby Walker, who became a big noise in Aussie soccer, died aged 86.

15 October 1959 . . . Former Bolton, Norwich and Brighton left half Stephen Wright died aged 66.

15 October 1996 . . . Former Coventry and Gillingham keeper Alf Bentley died aged 64.

16 October 1954 . . . Former Spurs forward Willie Newbigging died aged 79.

16 October 1959 . . . Former Derby, Watford and Norwich winger Fred Riddell died aged 72.

16 October 1996 . . . Eighty-one fans were crushed to death when 60,000 crammed into a 45,000-capacity stadium in Guatemala, to see a World Cup game against Costa Rica.

17 October 1943 . . . Former Newcastle player George Thompson died aged 65.

17 October 1947 . . . Inside forward Tom Fitchie, who played for Woolwich Arsenal, Glossop and Fulham, died aged 65.

17 October 1970 . . . George Sapsford of Man U, Preston and Stockport, died aged 74.

17 October 1975 . . . Former Ipswich, Norwich, Spurs and Hull forward and Hartlepool, Derby, Huddersfield and Norwich manager Cecil Potter died aged 86.

17 October 1998 . . . Former Falkirk and Bradford City full back John Whyte died aged 77.

18 October 1976 . . . Former Spurs player Matt Forster – 236 League appearances before joining Reading and Charlton – died aged 76.

18 October 1985 . . . Former Welsh international inside forward Bryn Jones – about whom it was asked at Question Time in Parliament whether the £14,000 paid for him by Arsenal to Wolves meant that transfers had gone beyond the bounds of sanity – died aged 73.

18 October 1998 . . . Former WBA and Bristol Rovers keeper Dick Sheppard, who played in all four Divisions, died aged 52.

19 October 1978 . . . Former Spurs and Brighton keeper Walter Bellamy died aged 73.

20 October 1982 . . . A reported 340 Soviet fans died in Moscow's Lenin Stadium when a crush occurred during the UEFA Cup Second round game between Spartak Moscow and Haarlem of Holland.

20 October 1985 . . . Bryn Jones, Welsh international inside forward, who when sold in 1938 to Arsenal for £14,000 by Wolves, was the most expensive player in the game, died aged 73.

22 October 1996 . . . Former Doncaster and Villa full back Vic Potts died aged 71.

23 October 1971 . . . Former Manchester City full back Albert Allen died aged 80.

23 October 1998 . . . Former Charlton, Fulham, Palace and Watford inside forward John Trevor Smith died aged 88.

24 October 1994 . . . Former Newcastle, Grimsby and Peterborough winger George Hair died aged 69.

24 October 1999 . . . Former Blackpool, Bolton and Stockport defender Gordon Kennedy died aged 75.

25 October 1949 . . . One of the few players to adorn a pub sign – he became a landlord and featured on the East Suffolk Tavern sign playing football – Arthur Cropper died at the age of 43, having turned out for Norwich, Clapton Orient and Gillingham.

25 October 1970 . . . Former Luton, Southend and Norwich keeper Arthur Purdy died aged 66.

26 October 1967 . . . Former Fulham, Bournemouth, Southend and Norwich inside forward Theophilus Pike – who scored direct from corners four times – died aged 60.

26 October 1965 . . . Former Luton Town and Norwich defender Bob Graham died aged 65.

26 October 1972 . . . Former Newcastle player Dave Fairhurst died aged 66.

27 October 1942 . . . Former Newcastle player Jack Dowsey died aged 37.

27 October 1962 . . . Former Newcastle and Norwich player Willie Bertram died aged 64.

27 October 1968 . . . Former Derby, Bolton and Norwich

winger Lionel Murphy died aged 73.

27 October 1977 . . . Former Norwich, Millwall, Notts County and Colchester inside forward Frederick Burditt died aged 70.

28 October 1970 . . . Former Newcastle and Stoke forward Harry Ware, who once worked, we are reliably informed, as a Saggermaker's Bottom Knocker, died aged 59.

28 October 1979 . . . Former Reading, Wrexham and Millwall wing half James Wallbanks died aged 70.

29 October 1933 . . . Former Newcastle player Joe Harris died aged 37.

29 October 1949 . . . Former Newcastle and Norwich inside forward Curtis Booth, who later became head coach for the Turkish FA, died aged 58, in Amsterdam.

29 October 1994 . . . Bristol Rovers, Gillingham and Charlton forward George Tadman died aged 80.

29 October 1996 . . . Former Blackpool, Barnsley and Carlisle half back, Frank Bokas died aged 82.

30 October 1969 . . . A winger for Luton Town with a reported 22 consecutive converted penalties to his credit, George Dennis died aged 72.

1 November 1957 . . . Former Spurs and Norwich half back George Pilch died aged 80.

2 November 1919 . . . A nationwide influenza epidemic claimed the life of former Newcastle player Bobby Templeton, at 40.

2 November 1994 . . . WBA keeper Harold Pearson, who succeeded his cousin Harry Hibbs as England keeper in 1932, died aged 89.

2 November 1996 . . . Former Everton, Brighton and Port Vale centre forward Cliff Pinchbeck died aged 70.

2 November 1998 . . . Winner of the County championship with Hampshire, wing half for Blackburn, Southampton and Bradford PA, Henry Horton died aged 75.

3 November 1996 . . . Scottish midfielder Gary Thompson, of Morton, Falkirk, Alloa, Dunfermline, St Johnstone and Forfar, died aged 39.

4 November 1993 . . . Former Burnley wing half Billy Morgan died aged 96.

5 November 1931 . . . Former Newcastle player Dave Gardner died aged 58.

6 November 1920 . . . A fire destroyed a 4,000-seater, wooden stand at Manchester City's Maine Road stadium – claiming a much loved victim, the club mascot Nell, an Airedale Terrier.

6 November 1996 . . . Seventy-seven-year-old Tommy Lawton died – he played for Burnley, won the title with Everton, was sold to Chelsea then Notts County, then went to Brentford where he became player-manager before being signed by Arsenal. He scored 22 goals in 23 England internationals and was never booked.

7 November 1987 . . . England full back Arthur Willis, who played for Spurs and Swansea, died aged 67.

7 November 1997 . . . Former Welsh international centre half – 21 caps – and Hereford player-manager, Ray Daniel, also of Arsenal and Sunderland, died aged 69.

8 November 1929 . . . Former Newcastle player Albert Shepherd died aged 44.

8 November 1962 . . . Former Barnsley, Norwich and Southend inside left Victor Whitham died aged 68.

8 November 1992 . . . Former Norwich half back Sid Earl died aged 90.

8 November 1993 . . . Former Spurs stalwart defender Arthur Rowe, who became title-winning manager at the club, buying Alf Ramsey, died aged 87.

8 November 1999 . . . Norwich, Rangers, Alloa, and Dundee United full back John Kerr died aged 87.

9 November 1974 . . . Former Airdrie, Brentford, Chelsea, Norwich, Carlisle, Cowdenbeath, Bury, Huddersfield and Mansfield inside forward George Anderson died aged 70.

9 November 1980 . . . Liberia were mightily relieved to manage a goalless draw against Gambia in an African cup game – having been threatened with execution by firing squad by the country's authorities had they been beaten.

10 November 1998 . . . Former Bristol Rovers forward John Baldie died aged 77.

11 November 1994 . . . Former Grimsby, Lincoln, Peterborough and Republic of Ireland keeper George Moulson died aged 80.

12 November 1974 . . . After South Vietnam had won a match, supporter Nguyen Van Thang, 27, reportedly died when a fellow fan celebrated by pointing what he thought was an unloaded gun at him and pulling the trigger – an action which demonstrated graphically that the gun had been loaded after all.

12 November 1998 . . . Centre forward with Norwich – hat trick on debut – Spurs – two on debut – and Southend, Roy Hollis, died aged 72.

13 November 1985 . . . Billy Lane, who in 1933 scored a hat-trick in three minutes for Watford against Clapton Orient, died aged 82.

14 November 1958 . . . Former Brighton and Norwich inside left Walter Smith died aged 84.

14 November 1987 . . . Former Spurs, Norwich, Hull and Bury player John Acquroff, who scored a hat-trick in a match at the age of 72, died in Australia aged 76.

14 November 1989 . . . A player with WBA, then Man U coach and assistant manager, Jimmy Murphy died aged 89.

14 November 1994 . . . Former Middlesbrough, Bristol Rovers and Bristol City keeper John Anderson died aged 70.

14 November 1994 . . . Ipswich forward Stan Parker died aged 74.

15 November 1993 . . . Former Fulham – 295 games, 51 goals – player Jack Finch died aged 84.

16 November 1931 . . . Former Walsall, Spurs and Chelsea player David Copeland died aged 56.

16 November 1985 . . . A former Norwich right half, called just William Brown died the day before his 83rd birthday.

17 November 1982 . . . Drunken spectators throwing firecrackers and bottles sparked the stampede in which 24 people, including 12 children, were killed at the end of a game at the Pascual Guerrero stadium in Colombia.

17 November 1993 . . . Wales supporter John Hill, 67, was killed when a distress rocket was fired into the crowd at the end of the World Cup qualifier between Wales and Romania.

18 November 1971 . . . Former Barnsley and Norwich player – for whom he played in their first ever League match – George Addy died aged 80.

18 November 1979 . . . Former Oldham, Norwich and Luton Town centre half Peter Burke died aged 67.

18 November 1990 . . . Former Norwich and Colchester left bank Ray Price died aged 46.

19 November 1957 . . . Former Newcastle player Jack Allen died aged 54.

19 November 1923 . . . The funeral took place of murdered Villa player Tommy Ball. Thousands lined the route to St John's Church in Perry Barr, where a granite football still marks the grave.

19 November 1965 . . . Former Newcastle player Tom Phillipson died aged 67.

19 November 1991 . . . Former Norwich and Bournemouth forward (Ernest) Leslie Eyre died aged 69.

19 November 1975 . . . Former Norwich, Tranmere and Halifax half back Joe McGrae died aged 72.

20 November 1975 . . . Former Newcastle player Robert Roxburgh died aged 78.

20 November 1998 . . . Former Walsall, Mansfield, Liverpool, Crewe, Gillingham and Chester winger Fred Morris died aged 69.

21 November 1983 . . . Francis Cassidy, whose Football League career consisted of one match in 1937 as centre forward for Norwich, died aged 66.

22 November 1990 . . . Former Norwich left half Richard Guy died aged 69.

22 November 1995 . . . Colombian international defender Albeiro Pico Hernandez, 23, of Club Envigador, was shot fatally seven times on his way to training.

23 November 1924 . . . Former Newcastle player Charlie Watts reportedly committed suicide, aged 52.

23 November 1952 . . . Defender Arthur Whalley, who cost Man U £50 from Blackpool in 1909 and earned them £1,000 when transferred to Southend in 1920, died aged 66.

23 November 1954 . . . Appropriately enough for a keen cricketer, who played that sport for Middlesex, Les Dolding was living at Hooking Green when the former Chelsea and Norwich winger died in a car crash, aged 31.

24 November 1931 . . . Former Grimsby, Sheffield United, Spurs and Watford player, Welsh international John L. Jones died aged 65.

24 November 1980 . . . Former Mansfield, Sheffield Wednesday, Notts County, Tranmere, Southampton and Ipswich player Jack Roy died aged 66.

25 November 1954 . . . Goalkeeper in Norwich's first League game, Herbert Skermer died aged 58.

25 November 1959 . . . Former Newcastle player Bob McColl, who founded a chain of newsagents, died aged 83.

26 November 1996 . . . Former Welsh international centre half Harry Hanford of Sheffield Wednesday and Exeter died aged 69.

28 November 1994 . . . Billy Hindmarsh, former Portsmouth and Swindon defender died aged 74.

28 November 1998 . . . Former Luton, Southampton and Colchester inside forward Augustus Scott died aged 77.

29 November 1976 . . . Former Norwich forward – albeit for just one game – Norman Cole died aged 63.

29 November 1990 . . . Former Sheffield Wednesday full back Ted Catlin, winner of five England caps, died aged 80.

30 November 1957 . . . Former Man U, Blackburn and Coventry player Alex Bell died aged 52.

1 December 1934 . . . Gillingham striker Sim Raleigh suffered a mid-air collision with Brighton defender Paul Mooney, but continued to play after smelling salt treatment, only to collapse during the second half. He was taken to hospital, where he died later that evening.

1 December 1967 . . . Former Norwich and Kilmarnock player John Aitken died aged 70.

1 December 1996 . . . Former Torquay, Manchester City and Charlton full back Syd Cann – who managed Southampton 1949–51 – died aged 85.

3 December 1941 . . . Former Newcastle player Neil Harris died aged 47.

4 December 1993 . . . Former Everton striker Roy Vernon died aged 56.

4 December 1998 . . . Percy Ames – whose career included a consecutive run of 230 outings in goal for Colchester from February 1956 to January 1961 – died aged 66.

5 December 1997 . . . Former Notts County, Coventry and Chesterfield inside forward John Marsh died aged 74.

6 December 1960 . . . Former Norwich, Liverpool, Brighton and Reading inside forward George Ritchie died aged 71.

7 December 1994 . . . Former Scottish international half back William Campbell died aged 74.

7 December 1997 . . . Having gained 54 caps for Scotland, former Leeds player and manager Billy Bremner died, two days before his 55th birthday. His ashes are reportedly buried at Elland Road.

8 December 1976 . . . Former Norwich and Grimsby centre forward Arthur Brooks died aged 85.

8 December 1981 . . . Bob Lord, local butcher turned Burnley FC chairman for 26 years, died.

8 December 1998 . . . Former Rotherham, Newcastle and Millwall defender George Bradley died aged 81.

9 December 1953 . . . Former Man U, Oldham and Crewe player Alex Downie died in his 78th year.

9 December 1971 . . . Former Spurs and Dundee player Alex Lindsay died aged 75.

9 December 1987 . . . Eighteen players and eight officials of Peruvian side Alianza Lima died when their plane crashed into the sea off Lima.

9 December 1993 . . . Former Spurs and Northern Ireland wing-half and Chelsea manager Robert Dennis Blanchflower, universally known as Danny, who once walked away from the TV programme *This Is Your Life* because 'I didn't fancy the idea', died aged 67.

11 December 1982 . . . Walter Bell, the first player to score two goals for Norwich in a Football League match, died aged 86.

11 December 1976 . . . Five people died during a Haiti v Cuba World Cup qualifying game when a soldier accidentally fired a gun, sparking panic. Afterwards the soldier reportedly shot himself.

12 December 1999 . . . Leo Harden, who alternated dustcart driving and playing football for Hartlepool – 170 League games, 47 goals – and was known as The Flying Dustman died aged 76.

13 December 1997 . . . Former Preston half back and later manager, Jimmy Milne died aged 86.

14 December 1918 . . . Newcastle and Chelsea player Angus Douglas died of pneumonia, aged 29.

14 December 1960 . . . Former Charlton, Gillingham, Bristol Rovers, Bristol City and Norwich inside left Tom Williams died aged 61.

14 December 1994 . . . Former Dundee United, Forfar, Falkirk, Raith and Montrose player Peter Cabrielli died aged 85.

14 December 1996 . . . Former Blackpool, Palace, Coventry and Plymouth striker John Craven died in California, aged 49.

14 December 1998 . . . Former Palace, Portsmouth, Coventry, Luton, Oxford and Colchester – where he helped knock Leeds out of the Cup – inside forward Brian Lewis died aged 55.

15 December 1930 . . . One of the most famous characters in football history died aged 20 – Billy the White Horse, who controlled the crowd which spilled on to the Middlesbrough at the first ever Wembley FA Cup Final in 1923, assisted by Constable George Scorey, appropriately enough.

15 December 1983 . . . Former Fulham, Exeter, Port Vale, Chesterfield, Gillingham, Accrington, Walsall, Darlington and Norwich wing half Harold Crockford – bet you didn't know he became a bookie – died aged 90.

17 December 1964 . . . Former Bournemouth, Norwich, Derby, Grimsby, Swindon, Port Vale, Newport and Chesterfield centre forward Ralph Hunt died aged 31, in a car crash.

17 December 1991 . . . Former Newcastle player Ron Starling died aged 82.

17 December 1993 . . . Former Leyton Orient, Arsenal, Forest and Millwall player Len Julians died aged 60.

18 December 1951 . . . Former Norwich winger Percy Barnfather, who won a First World War Military Cross, died the day after his 72nd birthday.

18 December 1998 . . . Sounding like a comic-book character, Harry Haddock, Scottish international full back with the longest throw in the game, died aged 73.

19 December 1998 . . . Former Dundee, Partick Thistle and Hamilton Accies striker of the forties and fifties Alex Stott died.

21 December 1935 . . . Former Newcastle and Chelsea player Ted Birnie died aged 57.

21 December 1996 . . . Former Ayr, Aldershot and Nuneaton wing half Wilf Armory died aged 84.

22 December 1964 . . . Plus-fours-wearing Major Frank Buckley who won an England cap, fought in the Boer War, was twice mentioned in Despatches, played for Villa, Brighton, Man U, Manchester City, Birmingham, Derby, Bradford and Norwich – where he was also manager, as he was at Wolves, Notts County, Hull, Leeds and Walsall – died aged 82.

23 December 1931 . . . Former Chelsea player Walter Bettridge died.

23 December 1943 . . . A flight sergeant gunner in the RAF, Arsenal's Bobby Daniel was reported missing.

23 December 1972 . . . Former England international Jimmy Dimmock, whose goal won the 1921 FA Cup for Spurs, died aged 72.

23 December 1964 . . . Former Derby and Norwich centre forward James Jackson died aged 66.

24 December 1952 . . . Former Derby and Norwich centre half Bernard McLaverty died aged 54.

24 December 1978 . . . Former Newcastle player Stan Seymour died aged 85.

24 December 1979 . . . Former Liverpool, Bristol City, Preston, Norwich, Exeter and Hartlepool inside right Thomas Scott died aged 75.

24 December 1996 . . . Player with Dundee and Dundee United, Robert Robinson, four Scottish caps, died aged 46.

25 December 1899 . . . Former Liverpool, Tottenham and Thames Ironworks (West Ham) goalscorer Thomas Harry Bradshaw died aged 26.

25 December 1909 . . . Hibernians' James Maine died from internal injuries suffered during a game against Partick Thistle when he was kicked in the stomach.

25 December 1992 . . . FA secretary Ted Croker died aged 68.

25 December 1998 . . . Former Southend, Portsmouth and Southampton wing half Tom Bushby died aged 84.

25 December 1998 . . . John McGrath, former Bury, Newcastle and Southampton centre half who became manager of Port Vale, Chester, Preston and Halifax, died aged 60.

26 December 1963 . . . Former Norwich forward Robert Collinson died aged 88. He also skippered Yorkshire at cricket.

27 December 1985 . . . The Alloa v Dumbarton Scottish First Division match was postponed after Erich Schaedler, full back for the latter, was found dead in his car, aged 36.

28 December 1983 . . . Promising player Peter Southey, who had made one appearance in Spurs' first team, died tragically aged 21, of leukaemia.

28 December 1999 . . . Former Bristol City stalwart full back Theodore Michael Thresher died aged 68.

29 December 1966 . . . Former Derby, QPR and Spurs player Charlie Rance missed out on an England amateur cap when King Edward VII died and on his only League goal for Spurs when the game was abandoned due to fog. He died aged 77.

30 December 1969 . . . Former Hartlepool, Rochdale and Norwich inside right John Stephenson died aged 70.

30 December 1994 . . . The first footballer to win a full England cap whilst at Bristol Rovers, Geoff Bradford died aged 67.

31 December 1962 . . . Former Brentford, Gillingham and Norwich full back Albert Frederick – known as Archie – Reay died aged 61.

31 December 1966 . . . Man U and England striker Joe Spence died aged 68.

31 December 1971 . . . Former Norwich full back Horace Ellis died aged 88.

31 December 1991 . . . A week after his 101st birthday, former Preston and Hartlepool player William Luke died.

31 December 1990 . . . Immortalised in the book *The Greatest Player You Never Saw*, Reading and Cardiff maverick Robin Friday died aged 38.

31 December 1994 . . . Former Bristol Rovers and England forward Geoff Bradford – 461 League games, 245 goals – died aged 67.

Bibliography

Appleton, Arthur. *Hotbed of Soccer*. SBC, 1961.

Ball, Phil. *Morbo*. WSC, 2001.

Betts, Graham. *The Gers*. Mainstream, 1998.

Betts, Graham. *Spurs*. Mainstream, 1998.

Betts, Graham. *United: Day-to-Day Life at Old Trafford*. Mainstream, 1998.

Betts, Graham. *The Villans*. Mainstream, 1998.

Blows, Kirk/Hogg, Tony. *The Essential History of West Ham United*. Headline, 2000.

Bolam, Michael. *The Magpies*. Mainstream, 1998.

Brophy, Kevin. *In The Company of Wolves*. Mainstream, 1999.

Cairney, John. *A Scottish Football Hall of Fame*. Mainstream, 1998.

Campbell, Tom/Woods, Pat. *Dreams, and Songs to Sing*. Mainstream, 1996.

Collings, Timothy. *The Luton Town Story 1885–1985*. LTF & Athletic Club, 1985.

Davage, Mike. *Glorious Canaries*. Norwich City FC Ltd, 1994.

Delaney, Terence. *The Footballer's Fireside Book*. SBC, 1963.

Dougan, Andy. *Dynamo: Defending the Honour of Kiev*. Fourth Estate, 2001.

Glanvill, Rick. *The Chelsea Who's Who*. Boxtree, 1998.
Glanville, Brian. *The Story of the World Cup*. 1997.
Harrison, Paul. *The St James's Park Encyclopaedia*. Mainstream, 1995.
Hayes, Dean. *Burnley FC: The Complete A to Z*. Sigma, 1999.
Hayes, Dean. *The Craven Cottage Encyclopaedia*. Mainstream, 2000.
Hayes, Dean. *The Goodison Park Encyclopaedia*. Mainstream, 1998.
Hayes, Dean. *The Molineux Encyclopaedia*. Mainstream, 1999.
Hayes, Dean. *The St Andrew's Encyclopaedia*. Mainstream, 1999.
Hayes, Dean. *Stockport County FC: An A-Z*. Sigma, 1998.
Hayes, Dean. *Tranmere: The Complete A-Z*. Sigma, 1999.
Hutchinson, Roger. *Into the Light*. Mainstream, 1999.
Inglis, Simon. *Football Grounds of Britain*. Collin Willow, 1983.
Kelly, Stephen F. *The Anfield Encyclopaedia*. Mainstream, 2000.
Kelly, Stephen F. *Back Page United*. S. Webb & Son, 1997.
Kelly, Stephen F. *The Old Trafford Encyclopaedia*. Mainstream, 2000.
King, Jeff. *FC Barcelona*. Macmillan, 2000.
Lerman, Richard/Brown, David. *The Blues: Day-to-Day Life at Stamford Bridge*. Mainstream, 1998.
Lerman, Richard/Brown, David. *The Reds*. Mainstream, 1998.
Lloyd, Grahame. *C'mon City*. Seren, 1999.
Lowndes, William. *The Story of Football*. SBC, 1964.
Lugton, Alan. *The Making of Hibernian*. John Donald, 1999.
MacWilliam, Rab. *The European Cup*. Aurum, 2000.
McColl, Graham. *Aston Villa: Illustrated History 1874–1998*. Hamlyn, 1998.
Mourant, Andrew. *The Essential History of Leeds United*. Headline, 2000.

Penney, Ian. *The Maine Road Encyclopaedia*. Mainstream, 1995.

Randall, David. *Great Sporting Eccentrics*. Guild Publishing, 1985.

Raynor, George. *Football Ambassador at Large*. SBC, 1960.

Reid, Gerard. *Football and War*. Sigma, 2000.

Sims, David. *Arsenal: Memories and Marble Halls*. Pavilion, 2000.

Smith, Martin. *Book of Sports Obituaries*. Macmillan, 2000.

Tibballs, Geoff. *Great Sporting Failures*. Collins Willow, 1993.

Williams, Russ. *Football Babylon*. Virgin, 1997.

Willmore, G.A. *West Bromwich Albion: The First Hundred Years*. Readers' Union, 1979.